D1590974

Annapolis
GHOSTS

HISTORY, MYSTERY, LEGENDS AND LORE

Stories and Photographs by
Ed Okonowicz

Annapolis Ghosts
First Edition

ISBN   1-890690-19-8
ISBN 13   978-1-890690-19-9

Published by
Myst and Lace Publishers, Inc.
1386 Fair Hill Lane
Elkton, Maryland 21921

Printed in the U.S.A.
in Baltimore, Maryland
by Victor Graphics

Typography, Layout and Cover Design
by Kathleen Okonowicz

Dedications

To Matt Rocco DeRose
Welcome to our family.
Ed Okonowicz

Acknowledgments

The author and illustrator appreciate the assistance of those
who have played an important role in this project.

For providing access to their sites and materials or granting time
time to be interviewed, we want to thank:
Mark Schatz and staff at the Ann Arrundell Historical Society, Inc.;
Carter C. Lively and Lisa Mason-Chaney of the Hammond-
Harwood House; Lynn O'Brien of the Brice House; Patricia
Dempsey of the Communications Office of St. John's College; staff
at the Annapolis Branch of the Anne Arundel County Library; and
staff at the information desk in the Maryland State House.

For their proofreading and suggestions
Barbara Burgoon, Marianna Dyal, Sue Moncure
and Ted Stegura. These good friends and talented readers play a
very major role in the creation of each of our books. We could not
do this properly without their excellent help and useful criticism.

About the Cover

The photographs on the book cover were taken by the author.
However, the excellent image of the facade of the historic
Hammond-Harwood House—featured on the back cover of this
book—was provided by Carter C. Lively, executive director, and
Lisa Mason-Chaney, curator/assistant director, of the Hammond-
Harwood House. Their help is appreciated.

Table of Contents

HISTORY & MYSTERY

Introduction

Those interested in folklore, legends and ghost stories always look to the past to find out what happened. They search for leftover clues of what had been, some remnants of what had occurred before—hoping to find slight evidence that something has remained behind, in a dimension we cannot see.

This information is obtained by exploring people's memories (oral histories handed down through generations); searching faded documents, out-of-print books and newspapers; examining photographs of buildings no longer standing; and visiting locations that look entirely different from years ago. Often these places are victims of progress, having been destroyed and later resurrected to serve as functional parking lots, busy shopping centers, cookie-cutter residential developments and prefabricated office buildings.

But Annapolis is different.

The green colored dome of the U.S. Naval Academy Chapel rises over the city, dominating the Annapolis skyline.

1

History and the past in the town still exist through the large number of functioning ancient buildings. Many historic dwellings are used daily as government offices, ongoing houses of worship, historic residences, commercial businesses, academic structures and private homes.

Whether it's walking beneath everpresent shadows of ancient domes and steeples, along uneven brick sidewalks or beside walls bearing information on historic plaques and monuments—visitors and residents in Annapolis can stand, literally, in the very footprints of our country's early history.

Experts believe if you restore a place to what it had been—or even better, keep it the way it was—some spirits from the past will feel very much at home. One or two might decide to remain or, at the very least, feel comfortable coming back to pay a return visit.

If so, some believe Annapolis, one of America's oldest towns, also may be one of the country's most haunted locations. Similar to my other volumes, readers will learn that this book is about both history and hauntings. You can't have one without the other. But in Annapolis, the large, ongoing concentration of living history tends to overwhelm first-time visitors and, at the same time, to become commonplace to long time residents and workers.

In this historic water village, each corner hosts old homes with real-life tales to tell. Its uneven, winding streets have strange stories to whisper. In this book you'll learn about some of these.

After reading, I hope you will decide to visit some of these sites with a greater appreciation of the strong connection between history and haunted legends—and give some thought to what unseen and unusual events may continue to occur.

Until we meet again, in our upcoming books about regional ghost stories and history,

Happy Hauntings,

—Ed Okonowicz
In Fair Hill, Maryland
at the top of the
Delmarva Peninsula
Summer 2007

A Summary of
the Town's History

Many of the legends and ghost tales are associated with the colony's earliest days. Since some of these spooky stories have survived more than 300 years, they are proof of the adage: 'They're not good because they're old; they're old because they're good.'

To appreciate Annapolis, it's necessary to understand how it came to be and the significant role the village played in the early days of our country.

The Indians were here first. To them the site of Annapolis was a center for transportation, fishing and trade, for in the 1600 through the 1800s—before decent road travel and railroads—waterways were equivalent to modern-day interstate highways. With its location near and along several rivers and creeks leading into the all-important Chesapeake Bay, the site was the perfect location for early colonists to establish a settlement.

Later the village would grow and—because of its widespread reputation as the region's cultural and intellectual center—be referred to as the "Ancient City" and the "Athens of America."

It's believed a band of Puritans that had left Virginia landed in the immediate area first, in 1649, establishing a settlement called Providence along the Severn River. When that prime location attracted more settlers and the population increased, the authorities established a new county named Annarundell, honoring the wife of Cecilius, the second Lord Baltimore.

This settlement, which came to be called Arundelton, continued to expand. By 1670, a 100-acre plot—located between what now is College Creek on the north and Spa Creek on the south—was laid out. In 1694, Anne Arundel Town became the

3

Annapolis' historic State House served briefly as the Capitol of the United States and was visited by George Washington, Thomas Jefferson and other early leaders of the country.

capital of the province, replacing the region's original settlement, St. Mary's City, located far to the south on the Western Shore.

This more central, northern Maryland location was along a direct route with the trade and political centers of adjacent colonies. The new state capital—at the northern, narrow crossing of the upper Chesapeake Bay—also was more accessible to residents and representatives of the colony's Eastern Shore. In 1695, the city's name was changed to Annapolis, in honor of Princess Anne of England, who would later become Britain's queen.

In this time period, the two circles on the knoll at the high ground of the city were established, and several streets exited this town center, marking the directions of a compass. The royal governor, Sir Francis Nicholson, directed the town's development, and he indicated the neighborhoods where certain classes of workers would live and also specified where government buildings and waterfront warehouses were to be located.

In the mid-1700s, Annapolis had developed into a trade and cultural center, reaching what some considered its "Golden Age." Costumed balls—featuring music, dancing and fashionably clad men and women—continued into the early morning hours. Government officials, entrepreneurs and wealthy planters, shippers and plantation owners attended these gala events. A large number of inns, restaurants and hotels catered to the steady stream of travelers who came to and through the capital city.

By the late 1700s, the capital's residents and officials were involved in the whirlwind patriotic spirit of the impending Revolution. In response to the British Stamp Act, Annapolis held its own version of the famous Boston Tea Party. In October

This cannon standing beside the State House was brought from England when the settlers first arrived on March 25, 1634. The historic artillery piece had been part of the Fort at Old St. Mary's and was recovered from the St. Mary's River in 1822. It was given to the state in 1840.

5

1774, the Maryland capital's citizens burned the ship *Peggy Stewart* in Spa Creek as a symbolic statement of opposition to the British crown and its import taxes and restrictive laws.

Three of the state's four signers of the Declaration of Independence—lawyers Samuel Chase, William Paca and Charles Carroll of Carrollton—all have homes in the town that still stand. The fourth signer, Thomas Stone, studied law in Annapolis and later lived in the capital.

Several of the large mansions, which are now public historic sites, reflect the wealth of the city's golden era. This can be noticed in the homes' interior and exterior architectural styles and attention to detail, as well as in the expansive and well-designed gardens surrounding these inner city estates.

Although no major battles were fought in Maryland during the Revolution, the capital was a crossroads for troops heading north and south. A major event was the passing of French and American troops in 1781, as these soldiers marched toward Yorktown and the battle that led to the end of the war. In 1783, the Continental Congress convened in the Maryland State House, and for a year Annapolis served as the capital of the new country. The Treaty of Paris, officially ending the Revolutionary War, was signed in the Maryland State House.

In the early 1800s, preparing for a second war with Great Britain, the federal government established Fort Severn along the harbor. While there were battles and invasions throughout the Chesapeake Bay, and a major attack at Baltimore Harbor in 1814, Annapolis was never invaded by the enemy.

But there is an Annapolis connection to the "Star Spangled Banner," our national anthem. The lawyer/poet Francis Scott Key was a graduate of St. John's College, founded in 1696 as King William's School, and the third oldest college in the country (following Harvard and William and Mary).

In 1846, the Fort Severn site became the country's naval school, which today is known as the U.S. Naval Academy. Because of Maryland's strong Southern sympathies during the Civil War, this naval college was moved temporarily to Newport, Rhode Island. At that time, Annapolis served as a site of prisoner exchanges between the North and South, and the city was a major hospital center, treating tens of thousands of ill and wounded soldiers.

In the following decades, Baltimore, located to the north, grew more rapidly and took over Annapolis' role as a major commercial, industrial and trading center. But the ancient capital, with its attractive harbor, historic homes and old-fashioned alleys and streets, has remained a center of government affairs and military training. Today, tourism, recreation and boating are among the major identities associated with the city's current political, artistic and cultural lifestyles.

Haunts

Is Annapolis haunted?

Many ghost hunters, writers and paranormal experts are quick to say "Yes!" Even long time residents, business owners, government workers and historic tour guides seem to agree, and some of them have tales of their own to tell.

Many of the legends and ghost tales are associated with the colony's earliest days. Since some of these spooky stories have survived more than 300 years, they are proof of the adage, "It's not good because it's old; it's old because it's good." Anyone seeking information on the spirits of Annapolis will discover brief mentions of ghostly incidents in several old books about the city. Other unusual incidents, and updates of handed-down tales, are found in many magazine and newspaper articles, usually printed annually during the Halloween season.

The topics of these feature articles include murders, executions, lost graveyards, accidental deaths, riots, unruly mobs, slave auctions and secret burials. The incidents have occurred in what today are historic homes, recreational open space, government buildings, stores and on public streets. But only some of the long-reported Annapolis ghost stories and unusual incidents are included in this book—there are, of course, many more.

The tales selected for *Annapolis GHOSTS* are the result of library research, interviews and visits to historic haunted sites. Some of the chapters feature old and modern photographs, as well as details discovered and pulled from old documents. But during the information gathering phase, several *historic* events that occurred in Maryland's capital city were found to be much more interesting than hazy reports of ghosts and shadows. As a result, half of this book features paranormal tales and legends, and the balance focuses on fascinating, real-life events.

The interior of Maryland's State House dome is the largest in the United States constructed from wooden pegs. It is believed to be the site of an accident that created one of Annapolis' most well-known ghost stories.

State House
Air Dance

Dance was busy at work, plastering the top of the dome, when he fell nearly 100 feet, crashing against the ground below.

Hundreds of years ago, the term "air dance" referred to the final action of executed criminals who were hanged and dropped through a gallows trapdoor. Desperately, their legs kicked out, searching for a sturdy surface to provide support and delay their inevitable death sentence.

In Maryland's state capital building, tragedy occurred to a workman who committed no crime. Instead, he was attempting to complete a job that would last for centuries. But of all the thousands of craftsmen who worked for many decades constructing the magnificent state capital buildings, the name Thomas Dance is most remembered—not for his fine work, but because of the tragic accident that took his life.

Here is Dance's story.

Bad luck and tragedy seem to have been associated with the site of Maryland's State House. The first building, erected in 1697, lasted only two years when lightning struck and the resulting fire damaged the structure. Fire returned in the early 1700s and caused more destruction. A second State House was finished in 1709, but it lasted about 60 years before more room was needed and planning began on a larger replacement.

Work on the third—and present—capital building started in 1772, but the war for independence delayed its completion until 1779. Today, Maryland's stately State House claims to be the oldest U.S. state capitol building still in continuous legislative use. It also has a more prestigious distinction, being the first peacetime capitol of the United States, and it is the only state capital building that also served as the nation's capitol.

George Washington visited the building to resign his commission as commander in chief of America's Revolutionary Army.

Tourists visiting historic Annapolis are drawn to the State Circle, where the State House stands. Certainly, a large part of this attention is due to the attractive building's impressive wooden tiered dome and acorn shaped top projecting toward the sky. The ornamental spire, bearing fluttering flags, is an identifiable landmark atop the hill in the center of the town, and it dominates the surrounding streets, monuments and buildings.

Once inside the state building, visitors are impressed by these architectural achievements. They find their heads tilted back as their eyes are instinctively drawn upward, toward the deep interior of the building's dome.

But some in these tour groups have no interest in the hand-crafted moldings, wooden pegs and artistic ironwork. They're hoping to get a glimpse—or capture a picture—of the State House's resident ghost—Thomas Dance.

According to legend, on February 23, 1793, Dance was busy at work, plastering the top of the dome, when he fell nearly 100 feet, crashing against the ground below. Over the years, there have been reports sporadically of a mysterious figure roaming the capitol grounds, areas within the building and, of course, at sites near the interior and exterior of the building dome—where Dance had been working when he died suddenly.

Several workers in the State House were asked to comment on tales of the building's ghosts and, in particular, about any known appearances by Thomas Dance. But no one could add anything specific to the old established legends. That was not surprising, since employees tend not to want to talk—on or off the record—with strangers about the supernatural.

In a 1988 article in the *Annapolis Capital*, writer Allison Blake referred to the deceased workman in the State House dome as one of the "most public haunts in town."

In the story, a visitor center employee explained that after Dance's accident, his wife and children were forced to return to England because the state government would not provide the family any compensation for the plasterer's death. There also are stories that years ago some employees responsible for flying the building's flags had sensed the presence of Dance's ghost near the exterior walkways beside the dome.

Despite no conclusive evidence—in the form of photographs or electronic voice phenomena—of the ghostly workman's presence, the legend of Thomas Dance persists nearly 215 years after his tragic death. Certainly, the plasterer has become far better known in the afterlife than he was while alive. And as the years pass, any sudden noise, gusty breeze, abrupt chill, mysterious shadow and unexplained event have been attributed to the unfortunate plasterer—who never finished his task on the state capitol dome because he took an unplanned air dance.

Interesting facts

The Maryland State House, built between 1772-1779, is the oldest state house in continuous legislative use in the country. From 1783-1784, it was used by the Continental Congress and served as the first peacetime capitol of the United States.

In the building's Old Senate Chamber, General George Washington resigned his commission as commander in chief of the Continental Army.

A black marble line in the floor of the lobby separates the old (1772-1779) and new (1902-1905) sections of the building.

This large flag displayed in the State House's Maryland Silver Room is said to be the oldest U.S. flag with 13 stars of eight points that are set in rows rather than in a circle design.

11

On some nights when the tower clock of historic St. Anne's Church strikes twelve, a ghostly horse may be heard moving along Main Street and heading toward the river.

Headless Men and Main Street Spirits

Accompanying the clip clop of invisible hooves against the cobblestone surface was the creak of an unseen wagon. Its rolling wheels seemed to compete with the sound of rattling chains being dragged along the uneven surface of the old street.

If it's ghost tales you seek, the narrow streets of old Annapolis may be among the best places to look. For generations and through the centuries there's been talk of restless specters that periodically have agreed to grant brief unannounced appearances. To no one's surprise, all of these manifestations have occurred during the peak hours of darkness, when vision is limited and imaginations enhanced by the shadows of the night and the amount of liquid spirits imbibed beforehand.

These unexplained reports have included sightings of headless men, hearing the sounds of rattling chains and howling dogs and even a glimpse of a wandering wraith.

Headless Haunts

Since nothing stirs the imagination and raises the hair on one's neck more than a headless figure, let's begin there. Of course, most of the time the mention of a headless horseman, or headless figure of any type, causes people to immediately utter the words "Sleepy Hollow."

Ever since Walt Disney's animated classic about the plight of poor Ichabod Crane, being pursued by the pumpkin wielding Hessian soldier in Tarrytown, New York, Washington Irving's story in the small New England town has cornered the market on headless spirits. But there are numerous headless legends told around the world and across the country. In fact, the immediate region has its own fair share of faceless frightening figures.

Delaware Revolutionary War soldier Charlie Miller roams Newark's Welsh Tract Road, where a British cannonball decapitated him in 1777 during the Battle of Cooch's Bridge.

In Dorchester County, on the Eastern Shore of the Chesapeake Bay, Bigg Lizz, a slave and Yankee spy, lost her head while burying a chest of treasure in Green Briar Swamp. She's said to haunt the area in her futile, endless search to find her missing appendage—and also protect the gold.

A bit to the north, in Harford County, a murdered peddler's corpse was buried without his head, which had been sliced off by a robber with a sharp sword. For years, his ghost appeared, tapping a cane at a spot on the ground. When residents dug up the area, they found the missing skull and placed it—and the spirit to rest— in the grave with the body.

On Virginia's Eastern Shore, a bolt of lightning disintegrated the cranium of the Headless Horseman of Ragged Point Channel. To this day, the still-confused spirit rides in an endless and fruitless head-hunting search along the banks of Assateague Island and across the shallow channel to Chincoteague Island.

There are two reports of headless sightings noted in Elmer M. Jackson Jr.'s book, *Annapolis, Three Centuries of Glamour.* The most persistent and repeated incident occurred in the area of Market Space, which began operating as an open-air food exchange very close to the town dock.

As expected, farmers and sellers of produce, fish and meats would arrive by wagon or boat very early in the morning to set up their goods at the market. About that same time of morning, fishermen and crabbers from the town would head to their boats, tied up to the pilings, to set out into the bay for a day working the water.

In the late 1800s or early 1900s, a waterman was passing through the dock and market site. Since it was dark and visibility was difficult, he paused upon noticing a man seated in the area. But as the waterman prepared to pass the lone figure and offer a greeting, the mortal Annapolis resident noticed that the silent stranger appeared to be headless—and was holding his face in the crook of one arm.

14

Without a word, the waterman turned and raced toward home, only to discover the headless man waiting upon the front steps of his nearby residence.

Depending upon the written source or oral version, the tale ends with the startled man:

Heading in the back door and hiding under his bed,

Rushing in the back of the house and telling his wife, who goes outside to check and finds nothing,

Passing out from shock and being discovered on the curb by his neighbors, and

Passing out and being awakened by his wife, who curses him for drinking so early in the day.

The second tale involves a young man walking across Spa Bridge at midnight, heading home to Eastport. As he stepped onto the wooden structure, he noticed a man some distance away, heading in his direction from the hill near St. Mary's Church. Thinking he might have some company while crossing the creek, the young man waited for the black clad stranger to come closer, but became startled when the advancing figure had no head. The young man beat feet at a rapid pace, moving quickly across the span, his feet slapping loudly on the wooden planks.

However, as he looked back the headless stranger seemed to float over the bridge's surface, making no sound as he glided along. When the young man reached the other side of the water, the headless haunt had disappeared—whether into Spa Creek or into the foggy mist did not matter.

Rattling Chains

Universally, midnight is recognized as the bewitching hour—a time when phantoms roam and strange incidents occur. On certain foggy nights, according to Jackson's book, when the St. Anne's Episcopal Church tower clock struck twelve, the sound of hoof beats would begin to be heard along Main Street.

At first, curious residents thought it strange that no horse was in sight, and they initially attributed the sounds to their imaginations or dreams. But as the sequence of events continued to occur, and consistently coincided with the final stroke of the bewitching hour, the residents listened more carefully and watched more intently for any sight of the phantom animal.

This old photograph shows an unpaved Main Street, as it looked many years ago, when sounds of the phantom horse cart were heard at night. The photograph below shows the same location as it appears today.

Accompanying the clip clop of invisible hooves against the cobblestone surface was the creak of an unseen wagon. Its rolling wheels seemed to compete with the sound of rattling chains being dragged along the uneven surface of the old street. Although human eyes could not penetrate the dimension where the sounds originated, residents agreed that the mysterious wagon seemed to pick up speed. As it arrived at the foot of the street, the horse's pace reached a gallop and all of the sounds suddenly disappeared into the river.

Those seeking a source of the mystery have speculated that a wagon filled with chains, perhaps carrying slaves, may have sunk at the river's edge. And on certain foggy nights, the phantom team of horses and wagon driver somehow return to re-enact their final, mysterious midnight ride.

The churchyard surrounding St. Anne's Episcopal Church in Church Circle is the resting place for several notable Annapolis citizens, and some of these graves probably were dug by 'Joe Morgue.' When the area was unable to accommodate the growing number of dead, those bodies were buried in nearby St. Anne's Cemetery along College Creek.

Tales of
Old 'Joe Morgue'

'It was such a character that gave a thrill of terror to the juvenile mind whenever he came in sight, for it was the belief of the children that if Simmons looked at one and said, "I want you," the day of doom for it was fixed.'

This is a tale of graveyards, dead bodies, an old historic church and names one would expect to find in a John Dickens' novel—such as Jeffrey Jig and Jinny Corncracker. But the primary subject of this chapter is a colorful character with the rather unusual nickname "Joe Morgue."

His real name was Joseph Simmons—a long time gravedigger and well-known town eccentric, who died in the summer of 1836 at the age of 100. In those days, when wealthy politicians, noted businessmen and local characters passed away, newspaper obituaries consumed considerable space, chronicling the life of the deceased. During that era, news reports of the dead read much like the pages of a 19th-century novel.

To offer a glance at the writing of days gone by, the exploits of Mr. Joseph Simmons are presented as they were shared in the August, 1836, issue of the *Maryland Republican*. Read on and take a peek into the life of a remarkable character and his antics that prove, indeed, that "Fact is more fascinating than fiction."

The Obituary

"Mr. Joseph Simmons, the oldest inhabitant of this city, departed this life on Sunday evening last, at the moment the church bell tolled for three o'clock—that bell which from time immemorial he had himself tolled regularly five or six times every day. There lives not this day a native of Annapolis, nay, hardly any one that has ever dwelt amongst, or sojourned without our borders, that will not on meeting his melancholy note, recall the well known sound of our church bell and the striking figure of the old man that has so punctually attended to the precise moment of ringing the hour ever since the oldest of us can remember.

"Ere the church was a ruin, on the spot where the present edifice now stands, old Joseph was bell ringer. Not one man that ever has been a member of the Legislature, Executive or Superior Judiciary of the State of Maryland, not a student of St. John's College, or a scholar of our humbler schools, but will remember the well know summons which his bell gave them alternately to duties and to relaxation. Alas! Old Joseph rings no more . . . .

"But it was at grave digging, that the deceased enjoyed the distinction of having held an office longer than perhaps any man

ever did, nay, possibly ever will do, in this State . . . . In that single field [cemetery] is buried all social distinctions. Long before this field, now studded over with grave stones, on many of which the thick moss of a former century has accumulated, was disturbed to deposit the relics of the dead, was this old man our grave digger. Of all the vast concourse in this grave yard reposing, his hand has prepared and rounded the graves . . . .

The entrance to St. Anne's Cemetery, where Joe Morgue worked as a gravedigger for decades, burying many Annapolis residents

One town legend suggests an old man—resembling the church's deceased gravedigger, Joseph Simmons, also known as 'Joe Morgue'—sometimes appears in the back pew and near the main entrance of St. Anne's Episcopal Church on Church Circle.

"When he had reached a centenarian's age, he was the object of interest to all. With his white hair flowing over his shoulders, his aged form tottering with the weight of years, his shackling step and the soberness of his occupation, he presented to the mind the apparition of Old Time himself, lacking only the emblematic scythe to make the picture complete.

"It was such a character that gave a thrill of terror to the juvenile mind whenever he came in sight, for it was the belief of the children that if Simmons looked at one and said, 'I want you,' the day of doom for it was fixed. Having occasion then to pass the aged sexton, the children were wont to don their most courteous graces, and with unusual politeness to simper in the softest accents—'How do, Mr. Morgue?' This nickname, and that it was one the children were quite ignorant of, always infuriated Simmons, as the astonished children found by the sexton's vigorous replies that they had missed their mark, and had produced an effect just opposite from what they had intended.

"The spirit of Simmons' occupation became more and more a part of him as his years grew apace. He had been known after somebody had offended him to pass an innocent gentleman on the street and to take a ghastly satisfaction in hissing at him, 'I'll have you someday,' in a tone that indicated that he thought, with him, remained the issues of life and death . . . .

The old carriage path winding through St. Anne's Cemetery

"One incident has come down to us that does not reflect his character in an enviable light. There was in Annapolis one familiarity called, 'Jeffrey Jig,' (from whom Jeffrey's Point took its name), who with 'Jinny Corncracker,' his wife, lived at the foot of Duke of Gloucester Street in a little hut so small they could not stand in it erect. Jeffrey periodically fell into a comatose state and was several times prepared for interment, but always awoke in time to prevent the funeral. On one occasion his resuscitation was deferred until he was placed in the grave. Then as the grim sexton threw in the clods of the valley, a noise was heard in the coffin. The bystanders said Jeffrey was alive. Hardly realizing, let us believe, that the dead was alive, Simmons continued to fill up the grave, tradition says with the remark: 'He's got to die sometime: and if he was not dead, he ought to be.' "

The Haunts

St. Anne's Episcopal Church was Mr. Simmons' charge, where he helped with the upkeep, rang the steeple bell and buried the parish dead. When the tall building in the center of Church Circle was first erected, the earth surrounding the structure was a much larger burial ground. There the gravedigger planted many of the city's notable citizens. When the Church Circle's boneyard reached capacity, the church and town graveyard was moved to a larger space near Northwest Street, along College Creek. Here Annapolis' funereal artist with a pick and shovel laid to rest thousands of the city's residents.

When he died, Joe Simmons was buried in St. Margaret's Cemetery. However, some say his image has been seen leaning upon his shovel near ancient gravesites, perhaps thinking fondly of days gone by. There have been other reports of a long-haired stranger roaming among the weathered gravestones that accent the silent, rolling hills along College Creek.

The back row pew in St. Anne's Church is another spot that has been suggested to catch a glimpse of Joe Morgue's restless spirit. There have been tales of occasional sightings of an old man in workman's clothing, sitting silently in the rear of the church. When people have approached the long-bearded stranger, he has slowly gotten up and walked out (and sometimes through) the entrance doors, disappearing from sight.

Immediately following his death, the body of Governor Robert Eden was delivered secretly to a craft, waiting at the dock at the foot of Shipwright Street, along Spa Creek.

Phantom Funeral Procession

Eden's friends expressed concern that his corpse might be the target of vengeful patriots.

While many old cities have haunted houses, Annapolis is also able to boast of its "haunted street." A version of this legend by Julie Bragdon was printed in the October 1984 issue of *Annapolitan*. It involves the corpse of Sir Robert Eden, the last English governor that served under King George and who administered His Majesty's Maryland colony from 1769 to 1776.

In June, less than a month before the signing of the Declaration of Independence, Gov. Eden hurriedly abandoned his goods and property and sailed back to England aboard a British warship, docked and awaiting the official's hasty departure from town, in the waters off Annapolis harbor.

After the end of the Revolutionary War, in 1784, the last royal governor decided to return to the Maryland capital. To no one's surprise, the former British official was greeted with varying degrees of enthusiasm. During his official days, Governor Eden had worked and had been friendly with both American rebels and English loyalists, so he still had some friends living in the city. Since anti-British sentiment was still high in the years immediately following the conflict, Eden was astute enough to keep a low profile and the former royal governor's final days in Annapolis were calm and uneventful.

But his return to live in Annapolis was a brief one. Within a year of his arrival, Eden died while staying at the home of his friend, Dr. Upton Scott, at 4 Shipwright Street. Eden's friends expressed concern that his corpse might be the target of vengeful patriots. To prevent desecration or theft of the royal governor's body, several of his associates decided that it would be best if the former British official was buried with little fanfare and in a less prominent location than St. Anne's churchyard, located at Church Circle in the center of the Maryland capital.

Under darkness, Eden's coffin was carried down the steep incline of Shipwright Street to the dock at its end, where the narrow road meets Spa Creek. Once aboard a waiting barge, the corpse was transported to St. Margaret's Cemetery, outside of town, for interment. But nearly 150 years later, Eden's coffin and remains were exhumed and brought back into Annapolis. Today, the last British governor of the colony rests in St. Anne's churchyard, below a decorative, elevated crypt, to the left of the church entrance, at Church Circle.

An ornate coat of arms accents Eden's marble-topped tomb at his final resting place with the following inscription:

The home of Dr. Upton Scott on Shipwright Street was the last residence of royal Governor Eden. The home also was the dwelling place of Francis Scott Key, while the famous lawyer/poet was a student at St. John's College. At one time, the historic Annapolis structure served as a convent. It now is a private residence.

Here Lyeth Buried
Y Body Of
SIR ROBERT EDEN BARt
Provincial Governor of Maryland
1769 — 1776
Who Departed His Life At Annapolis
September 2 1784
In Y 43d Year Of His Age

—

His Remains Were Taken From
The Sanctuary Of The Old Church
Of St Margarets Westminster
And Laid Beneath This Stone
By
The Society of Colonial Wars
In The State Of Maryland
June 1926

Some have questioned whether the body was actually reburied, and wonder if only his grave marker was placed in the churchyard. But there's a more fascinating story indicating the British governor's soul may not be completely at rest.

It's said a ghostly procession moves along the sloping path of Shipwright Street, recreating the original funeral walk that silently secreted Eden's spirited soul out of town. It's suggested that the slow moving march of wispy figures occurs on dark, fog-shrouded nights. Some think that they have seen Eden's slaves carrying their master's coffin atop their shoulders, following other spectral servants who are guiding the way with glowing lanterns.

Of course, the phantom procession makes no sound, as the participants' ghostly feet float silently along historic Shipwright Street, heading down toward Spa Creek and the waiting ghost ship—into which all those in the eerie death march slowly disappear.

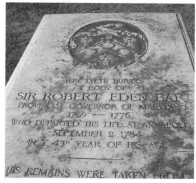

The final tomb of Governor Robert Eden stands in the churchyard of St. Anne's Episcopal Church.

27

McDowell Hall is the oldest building on the St. John's College campus. Its central location was used for public events and meetings throughout Annapolis' colorful, and at times controversial, history.

The 'Whistler' and Other Hauntings at St. John's College

One guard summed up the general feeling of many of the security staff that worked the night shift: 'You want to get out of McDowell post haste.'

E very college in the country is able to boast at least a few stories about its "school spirits." These unexplained sightings and mysterious events are passed along from class to class until they eventually take on a life and legacy of their own. Of course, as in the case of most ghost tales, some of these old college legends are also associated with historic events.

History

Annapolis' St. John's College, formally established in 1784, traces its roots to King William's School, the Maryland colony's free school, which was founded in 1696. The St. John's campus is located in the center of the capital city, near the State House. Originally, it was about four acres in size. McDowell Hall, the institution's central building, was opened in 1789.

Initially, the impressive structure housed the school's classrooms and library as well as living quarters for both students and their instructors.

Early students at the prep school and college included Francis Scott Key, who went on to have a distinguished career as an attorney. But Key's true fame is associated with his poetic talents. While witnessing the Battle of Baltimore during the War of 1812, the Annapolis school's most famous alumnus (Class of 1796) wrote the words to our country's national anthem, "The Star-Spangled Banner." George Washington's step-grandson and two of his nephews also attended this recognized center of Colonial-era learning. By 1806, St. John's College had graduated 105 students, including four future state governors, six judges and 21 members of the Maryland state legislature.

Annapolis' location, less than two dozen miles from Washington, and Maryland's role as a border state during the Civil War, both played a key role in the college's fate during that bloody domestic conflict. Many students left the college to take up arms and fight for their country. Some students signed on with Union forces and others fought in the Confederate army.

The war caused a dramatic drop in attendance and income; as a result, the institution was forced to close its doors for a brief period of time. Eventually, the Union Army assumed control of the campus and used the grounds as a temporary housing site for troops. Later the Army Medical Corps took over St. John's buildings, and the temporary infirmaries were referred to as the College Green Hospital.

When the college reopened it doors in 1866, the grounds and buildings were heavily damaged from the school's transient Civil War residents. No one will ever be able to determine the number of wounded troops that passed through St. John's College structures. But some suggest that the anguished spirits—of some of those who died in the temporary hospitals scattered across the campus—might have remained behind.

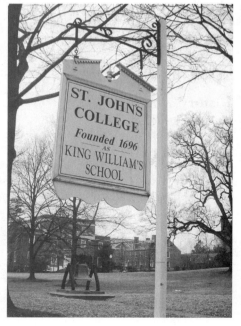

Haunts

Today, St. John's College occupies a picturesque 36-acre campus at the northern edge of the town's historic district, extending from College Creek to the area near the State House. Historic McDowell Hall stands at the top of a knoll, overlooking a spacious, rolling lawn. This 18th-century building marks the historic center of the institution. But some say within McDowell Hall and its old Great Hall, as well as in a some other buildings on the picturesque campus, a few restless phantoms may reside.

The 'Whistler'

In a 1982 article, entitled "The Whistler—and the wayward elevator," Becky Wilson, the college's former communications director, stated that some campus security guards have heard "the call of that tantalizing, bodiless 'Whistler' who sends shivers down their spine." For many years, members of the college security force, as well as some students, have reported hearing distinct whistling sounds that originated from an unknown source and indistinct campus locations.

One guard was "teased" by the musical phantom as the security official made his nightly rounds near the school library. In some instances the guard reported that the sound seemed to come from whichever side of the library building he had just left. On other occasions, the sound seemed to be right behind him and also coming from as far away as the gymnasium.

Another guard reported hearing the sound coming through an open window in the gymnasium. However, a thorough investigation of that building offered no evidence that would help solve the persistent mystery.

Some guards had suggested that the "Whistler" might be a student or a group of students playing a prank. But the sound also occurred while the school was not in session. This development caused the security force to discard that theory, and some agreed that the "Whistler's" presence during school breaks made the invisible tunesmith's melodies a bit more eerie.

Apparently, the "Whistler" can do more than just carry a tune. The mysterious melody maker also seems to be able to travel at an amazingly speedy pace. In a few instances, his distinctive sounds were heard at distant ends of the campus within seconds—much too far for a mere mortal to travel.

31

In a 1982 article in the *Annapolis Capital*, reporter Jacqueline Duke referred to the "Whistler," as an invisible, pesky wraith that "for years has teased guards by luring them from one end of the campus to another with its disconcertingly human call."

McDowell Hall

Given its long and, at times, tragic history, one would expect some mysterious entities would inhabit or be drawn to McDowell Hall, the college's oldest building.

In Wilson's article, one guard summed up the general feeling of many of the security staff that worked the night shift. "You want to get out of McDowell post haste," the guard said.

The list of unusual incidents reported in McDowell include:

Two guards noticed blinds being raised in an upper floor window when the building was vacant,

Someone was heard walking, with a crippled gait, in an upstairs floor,

The tower bell rang off its regular schedule in the dark hours of the morning,

Lights unexpectedly turned themselves on and off,

Voices and racing footsteps of children traveled across the upper floors, and

Doors slammed and furniture sounded like it was dragged across wooden floors.

According to Duke, " . . . many a guard hesitates before entering the old brick hall and none lingers for long once inside, convinced a phantom resident stalks the place during the lonely hours between dusk and dawn."

The cannon near McDowell Hall was used in the War of 1812 and dredged out of the Baltimore Harbor. The Peggy Stewart Tea Party Chapter, Daughters of the American Revolution, and the National Star Spangled Banner Centennial Commission presented it to the college on September 14, 1914—one hundred years after the Battle of Baltimore and the writing of the Star Spangled Banner.

Library and Dormitories

In Greenfield Library, formerly the Maryland State Archives Building, a security guard was in the empty building, taking a break and warming up from his rounds during a cold winter graveyard shift. While sitting alone about 4 a.m., he heard the sound of machinery moving. He soon identified the source as the building elevator, somehow being operated while the library was vacant and all the doors locked.

As he stood in the front of the elevator entrance, waiting to see who or what was inside, the doors opened—but the large metal box was empty.

Wilson reported the agitated guard said, "I know that elevator has been messed up forever, but on the off chance it wasn't that, I now will go through the library to check it. But I won't sit there."

Sarah Waters, a 1988 graduate, wrote a paper about, "The Otherworldly Side of St. John's." In her fascinating work, provided by the college Communications Office, Waters detailed other unusual incidents experienced by St. John's students.

A young lady residing in a second-floor room in Pinkney Hall in the 1980s, reported seeing a cadet in uniform march in through one wall of her room and disappear out the other.

In the 1990s, a student studying in McDowell Hall opened the door to a second-floor classroom and saw a man reading by a fireplace in a room decorated with 19th century furniture. Startled that she had intruded on someone in what appeared to be a private room, the embarrassed student immediately said, "Excuse me!" and shut the door. Seconds later, she realized what she

A military figure was sighted in a student's room in Pinkney Hall.

33

had seen and knew that it didn't make any sense. When the young woman reopened the door, the setting was a standard McDowell Hall classroom—and no one was in the room.

The apparitions of ghostly lovers are said to roam the banks of College Creek. According to Waters, the two apparitions are the sorrowful souls of a Native American college student and the daughter of a St. John's College professor. Forbidden to meet and see each other, one night the heartbroken lovers joined hands and jumped into the icy winter waters of the creek and drowned.

In 1974, a student reported encountering two ghosts on the third floor of the Paca-Carroll House, one of the oldest buildings on campus and located west of McDowell Hall. The story was reported in a newspaper article entitled: "Ghosts (Civil War Nurses?) haunt St. J. dormitory."

While living in an attic room, the student was resting and, while he was in a dreamlike state, he said he heard voices of two women in the hallway and a knock on his door. He said he was unable to open his eyes, but he could sense the visitors' presence nearby, recalled them asking a few questions, and then he heard the sounds of their departing footsteps.

From the archives of Ann Arrundell County Historical Society Inc.

In this historic photograph, the Paca-Carroll House is shown at left. It is one of the oldest campus buildings. In the 1970s, a student reported strange incidents in his attic dormitory room.

It's been suggested that the women might have been ghosts of Civil War nurses, who had worked in the historic house and dormitory when it was used as a hospital for federal troops. Another student living in the house reported hearing knocking on his door, but when he answered no one was present. The incident had occurred several times. However, within a few moments of each unexplained phantom knocking, a real visitor soon appeared.

Lost Graves

In 1781, during the Revolutionary War, thousands of French troops passed through Annapolis on their way to Yorktown, where they helped defeat the British in the final major battle of America's war for independence.

Some believe at least four unknown French soldiers, who probably died of disease, were buried on the grounds of the college campus, some-
where along the banks of College Creek. Different sources state that the unmarked graves probably are located near the French Monument, which was erected to honor these earliest of America's allies. There are reports that wooden crosses had marked the soldiers' gravesites, but that the fragile markers had disappeared sometime in the early decades of the 20th century.

The impressive granite memorial was suggested by Henry Marion, a Naval Academy professor.

The French Monument on St. John's College campus, near College Creek, is believed to be the world's first public memorial honoring unknown war dead.

35

The French Monument was dedicated April 18, 1911, in the presence of President William Howard Taft and French Ambassador Jean J. Jusserand. Also attending the dedication was Count Rene de Chambrun, a descendant of the Marquis de Lafayette. Baltimore sculptor J. Maxwell Miller designed the monument, which features a female figure and marching soldiers in the background.

The French Monument on the St. John's College campus is believed to be the first monument in the world ever dedicated to unknown soldiers. And somewhere in Annapolis, perhaps in the monument's shadow, rest a handful of foreign soldiers, buried far from their native soil, and whose names and location most likely will remain unknown forever.

The plaque at the base of the French Monument states:

Erected by the General Society
Sons of the American Revolution

This monument honors unknown French soldiers and sailors
Who gave their lives in the American War of Independence
And are buried near here

Dedicated by President William Howard Taft, April 18, 1911

"Our soldiers rest in hallowed ground in a friendly country.
To the Sons of the Revolution
I beg to express the gratitude of France."
—Jean Jules Jusserand, Ambassador of France

The memory of their deeds will live forever.

Credit: Much of the information cited in this chapter was derived from a number of documents provided by the Communications Office of St. John's College. The material is used with permission and courtesy of St. John's College, whose cooperation is appreciated.

Some security guards and students have heard and, in a few cases, seen unusual events in and around McDowell Hall.

Brice House, considered one of the most historic and largest homes in Annapolis, is said to be the city's most haunted home.

Brice House: Annapolis' 'Most Haunted' Home

'The most chilling ghost stories told in Annapolis years ago were associated with the Brice House.'
—*Hal Burdett,* Evening Capital

Information about the Brice House appears in nearly every book on Annapolis history. In tourist guidebooks and magazine articles it is among the most suggested places to see. More importantly, for our purposes, the Georgian-style mansion located at the intersection of East and Prince George streets—has been referred to as the city's "most haunted house" and as having "more ghost stories told about it than any other colonial mansion in Annapolis."

If not the most haunted, it certainly is among the largest and impressive homes in the ancient city. Trying to photograph the massive structure is difficult because its lengthy brick façade extends nearly the extent of the block. But in this case, bigger may certainly be better, since a larger home may allow a larger number of ghosts with ample room to roam.

History
Construction on the Brice House property began in 1767. Eventually, the original structures would be torn down or added onto, resulting in the present-day 30-plus-room mansion. Also on the property was a carriage house, stable, out buildings and gardens. Today the central portion of the building is referred to as the "center block." To either side is a hallway (called a hyphen).

Each hyphen-style passage connects to an end building (called a wing) standing at either side of the structure.

The building was built by a successful merchant and remained in the family for more than a hundred years. At one time it was owned by St. John's College, which used the mansion for faculty apartments. In the attic, exposed beams remain standing, indicating the dimensions of the apartment walls on that top level. The last private owner was the Wohl family, who restored the home and lived there until the late 1970s.

The International Masonry Institute (IMI) purchased the building in the early 1980s. For the last 10 years, the organization's administrative offices have occupied sections of the Brice House, using it for meetings, conferences, a research library and a central resource center for the organization's U.S. and Canadian members. In addition, the IMI works closely with Historic Annapolis Foundation Inc., allowing the organization to use the building for special events, lectures, public tours and educational activities.

Haunts

If some historic homes in Annapolis seem to take care to hide their ghost stories in the closet, such is not the case with the Brice House. In an article "Ghosts give 'living history' new meaning," by Allison Blake in *The Capital*, the writer stated, "Anyone who's heard the historic district's haunted tales—and is willing to talk about them—will tell you that spirits dwell in the Brice House."

In a *Sunday Capital* article by Bradley Peniston, the

This main stairway leads to the second floor, where several sightings have been reported.

40

writer mentioned that Betty Aronson, a ghost tour guide, stated, "The Brice House has the reputation as the most haunted house in Annapolis."

A check of county historical society files and library records served up a slew of newspaper articles about the mansion's phantom residents.

"Brice House ghost stories" is the headline of one *Evening Capital* story, and another edition of that paper attracted readers' attention with bold print declaring: "Celebrated Brice House Ghosts Now Believed Gone: New Owners Haven't See Single One."

With what appears to be an undying fascination with tales of fright and bumps in the night at the mansion on East Street, the stories seem to prove: "Where there's smoke there's fire." The following summary of some of the building's tales will illustrate why the Brice House has earned a top spot on many a ghost hunter's most-wanted list.

The Colonel

The last member of the Brice family was Colonel James Brice, who resided there in the late 1800s. According to many sources, the gentleman was murdered (or died of unnatural causes) in his stately home. By the time his body was found in the library, the master's faithful butler had disappeared mysteriously. This caused neighbors to suggest that the servant should be considered the prime suspect of the unsolved crime.

However, subsequent sightings of apparitions have been attributed to both the murdered colonel—who returns seeking his murderer—and the missing butler—who may be looking for his master's hidden treasure. Other reports suggest the butler also was murdered in the building, and that his still-undiscovered body may be buried in the cellar, bricked up in a secret passage or hidden in an old stairwell. If this is the case, the butler may be roaming to call attention to his limbo-like situation, seeking someone to place his remains in an appropriate final resting place.

Sightings

Legends of hauntings in the house earned some level of respect when a former Naval Academy faculty member, Allen Blow Cook, reported that he saw four spirits during his stay in the building. The professor lived in the Brice House in the late

1920s, during the period when it was used as an apartment complex for college professors. In a 1957 interview in the *Evening Capital*, the gentleman detailed his experiences.

In the middle of one night he said he awoke and saw the ghost of the butler standing at the other side of his bedroom. He said he also saw a man, assumed to be Colonel Brice, dressed in formal clothing. "He wore a plum colored suit, knee breeches, a lace fichu [cape] and a powdered wig. He was quite diaphanous and walked right through my bed," Cook recalled.

The professor said he also witnessed an eerie incident involving a Colonial-era couple arguing in the gardens, in the rear of the building. He said the man disappeared into the gardens between the Brice and Paca houses, and the girl returned into the home and paced loudly in the floor above his room.

In another interview, the professor said he once came face to face with a white-haired gentleman in a black suit—and the image "gradually melted out of sight like a mist" right before his eyes.

Reports of sightings and sounds occurred in this second-floor hallway. Mr. Brice's bedroom was located on this floor.

Another couple lived in the north hyphen section for 18 months in the 1950s. They reported their son and his dog were in a downstairs bedroom that led out onto the garden. One midnight the boy screamed and his puppy was shaking in terror, with its eyes bulging out of its head and foam dripping from the animal's mouth.

The boy said he awoke and saw someone standing at the foot of his bed. Thinking it was his mother, he lifted his hand to touch the visitor, but no one was there.

Skeleton and Treasure

There also were reports of tapping and knocking sounds—sometimes in a regular, Morse code, fashion—originating from within some of the building's old walls. Apparitions have been said to disappear in plain sight and sometimes drift through doors and walls. But among the most fascinating tales is a report of workmen, literally, finding a skeleton in a closet. This occurred during a renovation of the building, when workers are said to have discovered the bones of a woman, who apparently had been sealed up inside a wall.

Some people have speculated that the long hidden corpse probably had been a member of the Brice family, and that the woman probably had been insane or mentally ill. Rather than expose the family to humiliation and town gossip, as would have been the case dur-

ing that era, the troubled woman was kept out of sight and confined inside the home. When she died, the decision was made to hide any evidence of her existence and wall up the body. No one knew about her life or death—until the skeleton came out of the closet.

Buried treasure was rumored to be hidden somewhere in the Brice House, most probably in the dirt-floored basement. One workman doing chores in the cellar said he removed what appeared to be a loose stone, hoping to discover wealth and riches. Instead, he

This hidden, narrow stairway is located behind what appears to be a set of doors leading to a room or closet.

43

intruded on the nest of a spider the size of a grapefruit that he claimed bit off the handle of his tool.

In Elmer M. Jackson Jr.'s book, *Annapolis, Three Centuries of Glamour,* he writes that a servant in the building also tried to locate the hidden trove, but ran off when he said he was approached by a "beautiful blonde girl with a halo around her head."

In an *Evening Capital* article by Hal Burdett in 1992, the writer said, "The most chilling ghost stories told in Annapolis years ago were associated with the Brice House."

To get photographs for this book, I was given a tour of the Brice House by Lynn O'Brien, administrative manager of the International Masonry Institute, which currently owns the historic home. She has worked in the building for more than 10 years. While aware of the ghost stories, she and most members of her staff have never experienced anything unusual. But, she did admit, she had heard two interesting stories.

In the early 1990s, O'Brien said she was talking to a woman, who had known the last private residents that lived in the house. She said the woman had heard that when one of the family members was dying in her bed, she told the nurse there was a woman wearing old-fashioned clothing standing at the foot of her bed. The dying woman ordered the attendant to get the ghost out of the room.

O'Brien mentioned another more recent incident that involved the building caretaker, who usually stayed late

This large fireplace in one of the mansion's first-floor rooms features the artistic detail created by colonial craftsmen.

after special events to clean up the grounds and rooms. One evening, after an event was over, the caretaker was in the building alone and heard the sound of footsteps coming from the upper floors. After inspecting the area, he found no one there.

"Ever since that night," O'Brien said, "he leaves when the last person is ready to go, and he comes back the next morning to finish up what he hadn't gotten done."

In a 1957 Halloween day article in the *Evening Capital*, the writer ended the story with the following statement: "There have been, of course, countless people who have lived at the Brice House and who have never seen a ghost there. History-wise, Mrs. Wohl (the owner at the time) said her research has revealed a number of conflicting tales dealing with ghosts. She says she isn't afraid and from her point of view, there aren't any ghosts. There are just the stories about them."

That seems as good an answer as any—but it certainly won't diminish the interest in unexplained and eerie activities said to take place in the "most haunted house" in Annapolis.

For information: About the International Masonry Institute, call (410) 280-1303. For details about tours and special public events, call Historic Annapolis Foundation, Inc., at (410) 267-7619.

Some suggest the spirit of the builder's mistress roams the grounds and interior of this historic Annapolis home, known for its magnificent architecture, antique furnishings and formal gardens.

Ed Okonowicz

Restless Mistress of the Hammond-Harwood House

It's said there have been occasional appearances of her apparition—looking out from windows in the upper floors of the building and also strolling through the formal gardens.

It's well known that ghost tales and legends are most often handed down through word of mouth. But in some cases a literary work has been found to be the basis of a tale that many believe to be true. In the case of a legend associated with the Hammond-Harwood House, some experts suggest that one of the home's ghost stories may have been inspired from a passage in an early 20th-century work of fiction.

Stately Hammond-Harwood House stands at the corner of Maryland Avenue and King George Street. The structure is an outstanding example of American colonial architecture. Throughout the year, the building hosts visiting school groups, holds special public events and offers guided tours.

As visitors pass through the home's formal gardens and magnificent rooms, they marvel at the fine workmanship and attention to detail performed by the original builders. But, according to one legend, focusing too intently in one direction can sometimes have unexpected and unpleasant results.

Such, according to one story, was the fate of the original builder of the impressive mansion. In the article "Ghosts Haunt Annapolis," published in the October 1973 issue of *Annapolitan*, writer Dyan Manger described how the builder's care and exacting demands regarding materials and furnishings extended the construction, causing the process to go on for several years.

It's a known fact that most women don't like to play second fiddle to anyone, or anything, including a house. According to the legend, Hammond went about erecting what he was sure would be the most magnificent home in the capital city, but he neglected his fiancée. The aggravated young lady—who had waited patiently for years to witness the completion of the home—broke off the engagement. When the home was finished, the owner had an outstanding residence, but no one with whom to share it. Some say Hammond decided not to live in the mansion, and instead he resided in his country house, Howard's Adventure in Gambrills, Md., where he died and is buried.

But where most facts end, legends and imagination take flight, often in an attempt to make history more interesting.

A story, referenced by Manger in his article, began circulating that the neglected woman later changed her mind and returned to the builder, becoming the secret mistress of the house. It's said she would enter and exit the mansion through a secret path, using two keys that were buried beneath loose bricks in the cellar. "One key," Manger wrote, "bore the marking 'secret chamber,' the other 'secret passageway.' "

The mysterious romance continued for some time, and when the woman died her body was buried in a secret crypt under the estate's gardens. It's said there have been occasional appearances of her apparition—looking out from windows in the upper floors of the building and also strolling through the formal gardens. These sightings might be evidence of the lady's everlasting presence and her satisfaction with the excellent workmanship of her building.

During a visit with Carter C. Lively, executive director of the Hammond-Harwood House, I inquired about the legend, asking if he had heard the story and wondered if there was any substance to the tale.

The director acknowledged that various versions of the legend had been circulating about the town for some time. "To our knowledge it's not true," he said. "We have no evidence to either prove or disprove the story."

But it is correct, he said, that the builder Mathias Hammond never married. After a few moments, the current director suggested that a few elements of the tale—especially the details about two hidden keys, a secret passage and a secret chamber—

may have originated in a novel, published in 1931 by Doubleday, Doran and Company, Inc. of New York. Entitled *The Brass Keys of Fenwick*, it was written by Augusta Huiell Seaman of New Jersey, who was associated with St. John's College.

Lively added that he knows of no secret chamber or burial site in the manicured gardens behind the present day mansion. But, he noted as we concluded our conversation, "Our gardens are much smaller today than they were when the house was built. Originally, they extended all the way to the Paca House."

If so, one wonders, could there be a slight chance that the legend is true? Could the mistress of the house rest in a forgotten grave located somewhere beyond the present day boundaries of the estate?

As in the case of all legends and ghost stories, we'll probably never know the answers, or discover how much of the story is true and how much is fiction.

For information: About hours of operation, tours and special events, call (410) 263-4683, or visit the Hammond-Harwood House web site at www.hammondharwoodhouse.org

One legend says a secret passage was located in the mansion's garden.

49

Governor's Bridge, south of Route 50, is a short ride west of Annapolis. For generations, the skeletal span, located at the bottom of a secluded valley, has been associated with stories of accidental death, murder and devil worship.

Strange Tales at Governor's Bridge

Tales persist of murderers and mentally deranged hermits roaming the woods along the river. There also are stories of bands of devil worshipers seeking animals to sacrifice during secret rituals.

A baby tossed from a bridge. Screeching tires. Car wrecks. Creeping fog. Broken hearts. Mysterious screams. Secret covens. Howling during each full moon.

These and other eerie incidents have been reported on numerous Internet web sites and at campfire storytelling sessions about Maryland's infamous Governor's Bridge.

I first became aware of this well-known haunted site in 2004, while at a signing for my book *Baltimore GHOSTS* at a bookstore outside Annapolis. A young couple told me about their late night experiences at the site, and they urged me to include this eerie "haunted bridge" in an upcoming book. In the intervening years, several other Annapolis area residents, and ghost hunters, have shared their Governor's Bridge stories. One person suggested that a lost Indian burial ground may be the cause of the steady stream of reported unusual events.

Not surprisingly, over the last several decades the bridge's stories have been changed and embellished by different tellers, who often raise the level of blood and gore to maintain the interest of their listeners. And some have incorrectly identified the Maryland structure as the original site of the famous urban legend known as Cry Baby Bridge.

Legends suggest that the Patuxent River, flowing beneath Governor's Bridge, has claimed the bodies of accident victims as well as babies that have fallen off, or been thrown from, the eerie metal span.

But urban legends usually are not connected to a specific place. Instead, most reports of these modern-day tall tales are of the "friend-of-a-friend" (FOAF) variety. This means the teller often starts out the story with: "Now this really happened! And I know, because I heard it from my cousin's dentist's receptionist, who said she heard about if from her mother's boss, who just happens to work for the company that doesn't want anyone to know about it. But, I swear, I'm sure it really happened."

What makes the tales about this particular Annapolis area, ghost-hunting destination special is that Governor's Bridge is a real, identifiable place—spanning the Patuxent River, linking Prince George's and Anne Arundel counties. Plus, it's rather easy to find, since it is located on Governor's Bridge Road.

Approaching the "haunted" bridge from the Prince George's County, western side, the word "SATAN"—painted in red capital letters on a rusted road sign—catches one's eye. Driving across the metal span and parking along the wooded shoulder of the road in Anne Arundel County allows visitors to walk back onto the bridge and peer over its side. Standing in the secluded, backcountry setting, it's easy to conjure up images of the many terrifying incidents that have been associated with the area.

Following are summaries of some of the supernatural tales and unexplained incidents that have been reported on, near and below Governor's Bridge.

Travelers have mentioned sightings of a girl in a flowing white gown, standing in the center of the bridge, who seems to be waiting for a ride. Some people stop and invite her into the car, and she disappears as soon as the passenger door is opened. Other drivers are too afraid to stop and drive through the misty apparition, at which moment they have reported feeling a cold "death chill," as the woman in white passes through the length of the car—and nothing is seen in the rear view mirror. Later, when inspecting their vehicle, drivers find no damage and no evidence of the vehicle having struck any humanlike figure.

People have heard crying baby sounds, which seem to originate in the water below the bridge. Some believe a deranged mother had thrown her young child over the bridge.

Others say a baby fell into the water and drowned following a car accident. In both versions, the dying baby's cries float over the water surface at night, repeating the horrifying incident.

Some suggest the young child's restless spirit, whose life was snuffed out in its first year of existence, is trying in vain to be saved and return to this world.

Late night travelers have said they've rounded the bend, about a quarter mile before reaching the bridge on the Anne Arundel County side, and seen flashing lights coming from the center of the structure. Thinking that the presence of emergency vehicles indicates a serious accident, the drivers slow down their cars as they approach the river. Suddenly, the flashing lights will disappear, and as they drive across the bridge there is no indication of any accident, police presence or roadblock.

Tales persist of murderers and mentally deranged hermits roaming the woods along the river. There also are stories of bands of devil worshipers seeking animals to sacrifice during secret rituals.

Romantic couples, brave enough to park on the secluded road, keep a wary eye out for strange movement and moving lights in the nearby woods. Many a car suddenly has sped off across the bridge, leaving a trail of burning rubber— evidence of a hasty retreat caused by the threat of unknown activity in the woods.

Certainly, many of these tales are similar to ones reported for centuries at other Cry Baby Bridge locations throughout the country. They also sound very similar to the campfire

The word SATAN, painted on the road sign near the bridge suggests evidence of the area's popularity with cult followers.

stories told about the infamous "Hookman"—whose exploits and sightings have been associated with dark forested roads in almost every state and in many foreign countries.

But in spite of its reputation—or perhaps because of it—the dark wooded region around Governor's Bridge continues to attract teenage visitors seeking a weekend thrill, and also lure professional ghost hunters searching for photographic and audio evidence of visitors from the other side.

But remember, shadows and sounds of the night excite the imagination and tend to exaggerate personal tales of terror. People often see what they want to see. Each hoot of the owl becomes a werewolf's cry; and each rustling branch announces the impending arrival of the escaped mental patient with the gleaming silver hook hand, sharpened to a very deadly point.

But why believe what others say—or write?

For those interested in paying Governor's Bridge a visit and experiencing their own evening of terror, or to take photographs of the area, follow the directions provided below.

Directions: Follow Route 301 south off of Maryland Route 50. Drive approximately one mile south and turn left (east) onto Governor's Bridge Road. Follow the winding, narrow, two-lane road approximately two miles to the bridge—a one-lane, metal skeletal structure that passes over the Patuxent River. Since the lanes are narrow, be careful of oncoming traffic.

From the archives of Ann Arrundell County Historical Society Inc.

This 1911 photograph shows the ruins of the Curtis Creek Furnace, also called Marley Furnace and Dorsey's Furnace. The ironworks operation dates to the mid 1700s. By the 1840s it employed about 150 men. An historical marker was erected in 1965 about a half-mile from the site.

Ghosts of Glen Burnie

One of the slaves, who had been badly abused by his supervisor at the Curtis Creek Furnace, apparently had reached his breaking point.

The Glen Burnie area south of Baltimore, along Route 2 (also known as Gov. Ritchie Highway), offers two ghost stories that have survived the test of time. Like many legends, they also provide a glimpse of how the area used to be—before the construction of multi-lane highways, fast food restaurants, auto dealerships and modern government buildings.

Death in the Furnace

In the 18th century, Anne Arundel County was developing into a hub of industry, boasting such successful operations as furnaces, mills, and a brickyard. Several of the mills were operated as commercial businesses, but a number of farmers located throughout the region ran private milling operations.

Area laborers included freemen, indentured servants, convicts and a fair number of slaves. A story provided by Mark Schatz of the Ann Arrrundell County Historical Society Inc., has been passed down orally for generations. It

The historical marker offers some general details about the furnace industry in the area.

57

involves a tragic event that some believe occurred at historic Curtis Creek Furnace.

In the mid 1700s, working conditions in all small manufacturing operations were difficult. With no government regulations, all of the laborers were subject to the mercy of the owners and their appointed managers. As expected, things were particularly hard on the workers that were slaves, one of whom had been badly abused by his supervisor. Apparently having reached his breaking point. the slave decided he could no longer endure any more physical pain and mental pressure.

To escape his dead-end existence, which offered no hope of freedom, the slave committed suicide by jumping into the deadly furnace. Just before he plunged into the heat of the bubbling fire, the slave is said to have turned to his menacing overseer and shouted: "You won't beat me no more!"

A state historical marker—located along the northbound lane of Route 2, just north of Sawmill Creek and the intersection of Furnace Branch Road—offers a clue to the location and history of the furnace. It states: *The Curtis Creek Furnace, located on the south side of Furnace Creek, one-half mile east of Ritchie Highway, was established in 1759, and with a foundry built in 1829, continued to turn out high grade charcoal pig iron until abandoned in 1851.*

Few drivers along Governor Ritchie Highway are aware of the haunted history believed to have occurred in the region hundreds of years ago.

Treasure Tale

An ever-popular topic is one of long lost buried treasure. But what is a safer, and more confusing place, to search for hidden wealth than in a graveyard? To help treasure seekers locate the hoard, a mysterious light is said to appear in and near the rolling landscape of Glen Haven Memorial Park, located on Ritchie Highway in Glen Burnie.

According to Schatz, the cemetery and surrounding area were once a farm. One legend suggests that the former owner of the property may have buried a large amount of money on his land, and immediately thereafter murdered the servant or slave who had provided assistance digging the hiding place—proof that "Dead men tell no tales."

On certain evenings it's said a floating light appears in the area near the spacious cemetery—and at times on the other side of the highway—to indicate the location where the long lost valuables might be found. The only catch is that the mysterious glow only is visible at night—a time when few people, even serious treasure seekers, want to roam the areas near the peaceful cemetery.

The tower of the State House overlooks nearly every narrow street and alleyway in Annapolis. In a small bar, on a full moon night, a stranger shared an eerie story, then walked away and disappeared under the long shadow of Thomas Dance's haunted State House dome.

Graveyard Shift Incident in the Morgue

'It happened not too long after I was out of nursing school. I was working the night shift, from 11-to-7—the Graveyard Shift.'

Nearly everyone has a ghost story. Whether a person believes in restless spirits or not, it doesn't matter. True believers and skeptics alike have heard a family tale, recall a neighborhood legend or are aware of someone who has claimed to have had a "real life" unexplained experience. And often they can't wait to share their spooky tale and watch the reaction of others.

It was winter, early evening in Annapolis. The streets were dark. A cold wind was blowing off the water and I was waiting for my appointment in a small Main Street restaurant. That's where I had agreed to catch up with Marty, who lived in the area and who had called and said he wanted to share a ghost story that he said "had turned him into a believer."

Although I had heard the comment fairly often, the serious tone of Marty's voice over the phone, and his willingness to meet with me before he headed to his nightshift job, gave me the impression he was worth hearing out. Besides, he lived in the county and I was visiting on a fairly regular basis. I decided it was worth waiting in town a few extra hours to learn about his unsettling experience.

At 8 p.m., precisely, the wind seemed to push open the bar's narrow door and toss the arriving bearer of ghost tales from the morgue into the small front room. We exchanged greetings. Marty ordered a warm coffee, and we took a few minutes to get acquainted before we jumped into the interview.

Marty (not his real name) is a nurse. At the time of the paranormal encounter he worked for a hospital "somewhere on the
East Coast." That's as close as I can get. He stressed that he was
concerned about his present "job security," and "if this got out,
people would think I'm nuts or making it up. Plus the hospital
wouldn't be very pleased." Then he immediately added, "But I'm
not making any part of this up. Everything I am going to tell you
really happened, and it changed my whole outlook on this
stuff."

"This stuff being?" I asked, making sure we were on the
same page. To which Marty did not reply. So I added, "As in
ghosts and things that go bump in the night, or strange things
that we can't see."

"Right. Those things like that." he agreed while nodding.
That was the best reply I was going to get, since, like many people, Marty felt awkward even uttering the word "ghosts." To him,
speaking the one-syllable, highly charged term was like cursing
in church in front of your parents, or even worse—saying something that some self-appointed speech sentinel might consider to
be politically incorrect.

I assured him he'd get used to his newfound vocabulary. At
that very moment, a waiter dropped a tray and the falling glass-
ware and dishes sounded like an explosion. Everyone froze and
stared at the embarrassed worker, then Marty slowly turned
toward me.

"That's a sign, right?" Marty asked, only half joking.

"Of course," I said, holding back a laugh.

"Good or bad?" he wondered, obviously seeking the positive
answer.

"Depends," I replied, shrugging my shoulders.

"On what?" Marty pressed, obviously nervous and seeking
some type of reassurance. I mean, this guy was tense, like the
rusty spring on an old, wind-up alarm clock.

"Lots of things," I said, "but look, you've got to relax. Take it
easy. This isn't like going to the dentist. It won't hurt. We're just
going to talk. I'll take some notes, and then . . . . "

"No tape recorders, right? I mean, I don't want my voice on
tape. And no pictures, either!"

By this time the guy was making me skittish. "Easy! Please.
Marty, take a deep breath. That's fine. No tapes or camera."

Laughing, I opened my arms and said, "You want to check me for a wire? Go ahead."

He laughed a little, and that sort of broke the ice. I reassured him, for the fourth or fifth time, that I would not reveal his real name or the name of the hospital. It took a fair amount of time to get him to settle down. After he made a quick trip to the men's room and ordered another cup of coffee, he seemed ready to go. And once he started talking he was a different person. The details of his story flowed, and any hesitancy seemed to evaporate. It was obvious Marty had been keeping the strange incident to himself for quite some time.

"Twelve years, almost," he admitted. "It feels good to finally let it out."

Shifting himself into a hunched-forward, arms-on-the-table position, he said, "It happened not too long after I was out of nursing school. I was working the night shift, from 11-to-7."

"The graveyard shift," I said, smiling. "That's good."

Marty chuckled softly, "Yeah. I've thought of that a lot over the years. Imagine if I hadn't been on that rotation. I never would have seen it happen."

Part of his duties, he said, was to take the bodies of those who died on his floor down to the underground morgue and place them in refrigerated vaults. On some nights, there could be several trips to the hospital's subterranean level, which was only accessible through a single set of double doors.

"That's important," Marty said. "There were no other doors, no windows, no way anyone or anything could enter or leave the area. Only one set of stainless steel doors, and I passed through them a lot of times with a dead body on the cart."

On this particular evening, Marty was pushing the corpse of an older lady—let's call her Gladys—into the morgue. He was accompanied by Scott, a friend who also worked as a nurse on the same general nursing care floor. His friend was having a rare experience—a slow night—and decided to tag along and take a walk, to get a little exercise, on the way to the "dead zone."

"When we pushed Gladys into the morgue," Marty said, "there was a guy there, standing by a metal table. He was waiting for us. He said he had an order to fill, and that he was going to remove the dead person's corneas, since they were needed for a transplant operation."

This was a common occurrence, Marty explained. People who donate their organs for use after death don't really think about the process and what happens after they die. But the harvesting has to occur rather quickly. That's why the eye technician was waiting when the two nurses arrived.

"He said it was going to take about 20 minutes to get the lady ready for the procedure, and he invited me and Scott to stay and watch."

Since they had a second body to pick up and deliver back to the morgue, the two nurses said they would return to observe the procedure. They figured it would be beneficial to learn about transplant preparations.

When they returned, Marty said, "We got to see a lot more than the operation."

Marty explained that the eye tech had prepared Gladys, the deceased, and as he conducted each procedure, he explained what he was doing to Marty and Scott. The tech told them how the corneas would be removed and preserved for transport in two small vials filled with red liquid, which he had set up on a table located about 12 feet away from the corpse.

"Everything was going fine," Marty said, "and the operation was fascinating, especially since we had never seen it done before. But then the whole attitude, and even the atmosphere of the room, changed and it became very uncomfortable."

Shaking his head as he recalled the incident, Marty said that the technician suddenly began to talk to Gladys, the dead woman. "He started joking and becoming really unprofessional. I looked over at Scott, and I could tell by the look in his eyes that he was bothered by it, too."

When I pressed Marty to explain what he meant, he said the eye technician pointed to Gladys and made comments about her unsightly appearance, about her excess weight, about the wrinkles on her face and body.

Marty hesitated. It was apparent he was embarrassed that he had been in the room at the time. I could see that he found it difficult to talk about the eye technician's rude comments and unprofessional behavior.

"The lady was older," Marty said, "in her late fifties or sixties. At one time she probably had been attractive, but that fades with time, for everybody. We're only young and fit for so long.

"There was no practical reason for this guy to make fun of her. Scott and I agreed. We talked about it a lot later. It wasn't just a matter of this guy disrespecting the dead. This eye tech was just a creep, the kind of weasel you know in high school, and when you run into him later you find that, like you expected, he never grew up. Once a jerk, always a jerk. I remember thinking, *If his company knew how he was acting, they would fire him.* But who would ever know what goes on in a morgue? It's not like they have people monitoring you there. It's not the kind of place where people are dying to get a job."

Realizing the unintended humor in his statement, Marty looked up and we laughed lightly, breaking the seriousness of the mood.

Getting to the climax of the story, Marty recalled how the technician had removed the corneas and placed them in the preservative fluids in small glass vials. All the time, he acted like a pompous college professor, expounding on his extensive knowledge of transplants and how he was the best at his job. He bragged that the owner of the company had selected him for the most sensitive and difficult cases.

"He even held up his cell phone to show us that he had the owner's private line on speed dial," Marty said, rolling his eyes. "Like we could care less."

By then he was wrapping up his procedure and had dropped the corneas in the glass vials and sealed and labeled them, writing the name, date and time. As we prepared to roll Gladys into a refrigerated chamber, the guy put out his hand and stopped the gurney.

Then, Marty said, "the mood changed sour again. He started up with his trash talk again, about how ugly the lady was and then he asked us, 'Can you imagine what the person who gets this ugly duckling's eyes would think if she knew that they came from someone who had a face like a sick dog?' "

Marty said he and Scott just stood there. Disgusted. They had had enough and Scott told the eye tech to get out of his way and out of his morgue. Slowly, the two nurses began to push Gladys away from the area.

Sensing their annoyance, the tech shrugged his shoulders and snapped, "Hey! Lighten up. Can't you two take a joke?" And he turned to walk toward the glass vials he had left sitting on the metal surface across the room.

"They were in my direct line of sight," Marty said, staring at me a few seconds. "Scott saw it happen, too. Before the technician was half way to the sealed containers, his case of instruments and the two vials, that he had sealed a few moments before, they all flew across the room and smashed into the wall. Hundreds of pieces of glass and tissue fell to the floor. There was a red fluid stain against the wall.

"The guy turned to us. He was in shock. Not only that, there was fear in his eyes. Total fear. I think he realized, at that minute, that Gladys—or her soul or spirit or whatever—had heard every stupid rotten thing he said. It was like she was sending him a message, giving him a sign. I'm sure he would never say, or even think, a bad thing about the dead, ever again. It was a life-changing experience for all of us, to different degrees."

Marty said he and Scott stopped and watched the guy run across the room, screaming, "Did you see that? Did you see what happened?" Then he turned to the two nurses, from his kneeling position on the floor, trying to salvage whatever he could of the disaster. But it was a useless effort. "It wasn't my fault. You know it wasn't my fault. I didn't do anything. I didn't touch them. I was nowhere near them."

Marty's eyes met mine. After a few more seconds of silence, he smiled and said, "That's when Scott, the guy I was with, looked at the creep and said, 'Hey! Lighten up. Can't you take a joke?' "

"To this day, and until I die, I know it was Gladys. There's no other explanation. She heard him. She got back at him from the beyond or wherever she was. I swear, from that moment on, my whole perspective on believing in the hereafter changed. It's also affected how I conduct myself around the dead. I'm more respectful. Now I know there's more than just here. They're out there, even if for just a short time after they die. They're out there, and no one can convince me of anything different."

We nodded. There was nothing to say. I let the silence work, waited for Marty to add anything else he thought might be important. He looked up and added that about six months later he walked into the morgue with a corpse, and there was another eye technician waiting to do a similar procedure. After a few introductory comments, Marty said he asked the new person if she could offer any information about the technician who had worked on Gladys' botched procedure a half-year earlier.

"The person told me, 'That guy's long gone. I heard he messed up a simple operation. Cost the company nearly eight thousand dollars. And he had no excuse for what happened. Can you imagine? He couldn't even offer a sensible explanation. But somebody who knows somebody said the guy claimed his vials 'flew across the room, like somebody picked them up and threw them against a wall.' Can you image coming up with that as an excuse?"

Marty shook his head, held onto his long neck with two hands and fell backwards against his chair. As I looked at him, almost exhausted from reliving the horrifying incident, I recalled a quote that explains why people usually fall into two categories when it comes to the supernatural: "For those who believe, no explanation is necessary. For those who don't believe, no explanation is satisfactory."

Sometimes it takes a shocking and unexpected experience, such as Marty's encounter in the morgue, to move a person from one side to the other.

The entrance gate of Annapolis National Cemetery is on West Street, near the circle at the intersection with Taylor Avenue.

Murdered Russian Sailor Buried in Annapolis National Cemetery

The Bivouac of the Dead
by Theodore O'Hara

The muffled drum's sad roll has beat
The soldier's last tattoo;
No more on life's parade shall meet
That brave and fallen few.
On Fame's eternal camping-ground
Their silent tents are spread,
And Glory guards, with solemn round,
The bivouac of the dead.

In the midst of Maryland's capital city—silent in the shadows of modern office buildings, and often unnoticed by passers-by rushing to appointments or traveling toward home from work—stands the hallowed ground of Annapolis National Cemetery. Like its more famous and larger Virginia counterpart, Arlington National Cemetery, this Maryland burial site contains the remains of U.S. service members and their families.

The small, four-acre plot was established in 1862 by President Abraham Lincoln, making it one of the original 14 national cemeteries and one of the oldest such national sites in the country. There are currently nearly 3,000 burials among the gently sloping hills and low valley.

Many of the original bodies in Annapolis National Cemetery came from deaths at nearby Civil War hospitals, established when Annapolis hosted both Union and Confederate wounded troops. Disease from epidemics of smallpox periodically swept through these area encampments. Other major causes of death

69

A view of the rolling hillside shows some of the nearly 3,000 gravesites in Annapolis National Cemetery.

included typhoid fever, chronic diarrhea (dysentery), consumption and tuberculosis. The two-dozen Confederate prisoners of war who died while in Union captivity can be found in the cemetery by looking for gravestones with slightly pointed, as opposed to rounded, tops.

More than 200 of the bodies in the Annapolis cemetery's graves are marked "Unknown U.S. Soldier." Many of these marble markers line the narrow paved path that leads to the tall flagpole in the center of the grounds.

Foreign Burial

One grave in Annapolis National Cemetery does not contain the body of a member of the armed forces or a family member. Nor does the white granite stone bear the name of a noted Annapolis or Maryland politician. Instead, Grave #2420, in Section G, is the resting place of a foreigner—N. Demidoff, a Russian seaman who was killed in Annapolis on February 4, 1864.

The visiting sailor was serving on the Russian man-of-war *Almay*, which was docked in the town harbor while on a good-will tour of the United States. With winter ice blocking the Potomac River and making the city of Washington inaccessible by water, the *Almay* crew was waiting for warmer weather that would allow the crew to set sail. Seeking entertainment, sailors from the Russian ship wandered through Annapolis' streets.

With the Civil War still raging in full force, Union troops patrolled the tense city, constantly on the lookout for Confederate spies and Southern troublemakers. As a state with strong Southern sympathies, many of Maryland's sons headed south to fight for the Rebel cause, with entire Maryland units operating out of nearby Virginia. While Maryland officially remained a Northern border state, a strong portion of the Free State's heart and soul stirred to the musical sounds of "Dixie."

The ongoing war had strained tempers to such a breaking point in this volatile border state that military officials had temporarily moved the naval college (predecessor of the current U.S. Naval Academy) north to Newport, Rhode Island. Indeed, Annapolis, during the latter years of the Civil War, was both a dangerous and deadly town.

On a cold winter evening, not far from the city dock, Demidoff and his shipmates were making the rounds, sampling the tastes of several the town's ample number of saloons. When a bartender at one watering hole refused to serve the foreigners, the Russians began to argue. Federal troops, who were in the saloon at the time, intervened to help the pub owner remove the drunken foreign sailors from the premises. However, once outside words were exchanged, tempers flared and during a subsequent fight the sailor Demidoff was shot and killed.

The Maryland Legislature, responding to a formal complaint about the incident from the Russian Embassy, launched an investigation, which its said even attracted the attention of President

A Russian seaman rests among thousands of U.S. veterans.

71

Lincoln—who was busy working on a much more pressing issue, the conduct of the Civil War. Eventually, the Russian diplomats and Demidoff's shipmates were apparently pacified. A week after the killing, both American and Russian officials, along with military personnel and townspeople, attended a religious Greek rite service at the naval school chapel, marched in the funeral procession through town and silently witnessed Demidoff's official gravesite ceremony and burial in Annapolis National Cemetery.

Directions and the Poem

The Annapolis National Cemetery, established in 1862, is located at the intersection of West Street and Taylor Avenue. From Church Circle, travel away from town on West Street. As you drive west through the circle, the entrance to the National Cemetery is on the right. There are two small iron field guns in front of the lodge building, to the right of the iron entrance gates.

The tops of the graves of Confederate soldiers have slight points, whereas the Union stones are rounded.

On a small metal plaque beside the cannons, is the first stanza from "The Bivouac of the Dead." The poem was written by Theodore O'Hara. While serving as an officer in the Mexican War, he was inspired to write his poem when he saw the remains of his fellow Kentucky soldiers—who had died at the Battle of Buena Vista, in 1847—being exhumed for their return to their native state soil.

During the Civil War, Colonel O'Hara served in the Confederate army with an Alabama regiment. These opening lines of his most famous poem are inscribed over the entrances of several national cemeteries.

For information about the Annapolis National Cemetery, call Baltimore National Cemetery at 410 644-9696.

Along Routes 50 and 301, north of Annapolis, a green highway exit sign directs travelers toward Parole. Many don't realize that the small town with an unusual name played an important role during the Civil War.

Camp Parole, Annapolis' Link with the Civil War

One's imagination tends to wonder what amount of human remains might rest beneath modern housing developments and highways, shopping centers and schools in the area that was known as Camp Parole.

There were no land or sea battles at Annapolis during any of our country's wars, including the Revolution. When British raiders traveled throughout the Chesapeake Bay, burning some towns entirely to the ground during the War of 1812, the Maryland capital again was spared from attack.

In the Civil War, the city's major role was as an exchange center of both Union and Confederate prisoners. This transfer practice—known as paroling—began during the War of 1812. It was done to reduce the captors' expense of holding, treating and feeding the opponent's troops for extended periods of time.

Because of its excellent harbor and the town's central geographic location along the border between the opposing sides, Yankee captives, paroled from prison camps in the South, were returned to the Union and deposited at the Annapolis docks. A much smaller number of Rebel prisoners that were released and heading south also found their way to temporary hospital facilities in Maryland's capital.

While waiting to recuperate—before heading for home or to rejoin their units—injured and ill troops were housed in a variety of locations. These sites included available space in city hospitals, temporary infirmary buildings, available room on the nearby naval college grounds and in farm fields and town open spaces.

75

John Settle died at Parole Camp in 1863 at the age of 18. His body is buried in Annapolis National Cemetery.

Facilities at the nearby naval college, established in 1846 at former Fort Severn, also were used to treat the injured, since the naval college and its students were moved to Newport, Rhode Island, during the Civil War.

The campus of St. John's College, at the edge of town and bordering College Creek, also became a major center for the sick, with wounded paroled Union prisoners from the South housed in the school's buildings and also in tents erected throughout the College Green.

The number of parolees at the college eventually reached more than 3,000. To keep the soldiers away from the temptations of the

Some of the graves marked 'Unknown' in Annapolis National Cemetery are from deaths that occurred at Camp Parole. There are more than 200 'Unknown' grave sites in the small, four-acre site.

city, some of the men were transferred to temporary quarters on the banks of the South River.

But as thousands of additional troops arrived, more room was needed. Camps were hastily established on a farm southwest of town. In only a few months, up to 20,000 men were encamped there. During the winter of 1862-1863, the paroled soldiers suffered from bitter cold and many became ill.

Frequently, there were reports of soldiers from the camp straying into Annapolis, where they got involved in arguments with the locals and terrified the residents. The commander of Camp Parole restricted access to Annapolis, canceling passes into town, and even forbidding gambling and drinking of liquor. In a September 1944, Baltimore *Morning Sun* article about Parole, the author mentioned rumors of soldiers that were robbed, beaten and murdered in their sleep, with some being buried in unmarked graves in and around the camp during the night.

Cavalry troops were assigned to the camp to help maintain order, capture deserters and prevent wandering troops from bothering local farmers, area residents and city merchants.

In the fall of 1863, the Army constructed buildings and named the area Parole Barracks. This area grew to more than 50 barracks buildings and was named Camp Parole, which lasted until the end of the Civil War. It's estimated that nearly 70,000

This old artwork shows the large size of the Civil War camp at Parole, where tens of thousands of troops were housed during the Civil War. A major shopping mall complex is being constructed at the site.

77

prisoners, awaiting parole, were processed through Camp Parole, which was closed and disbanded in the fall of 1865.

Other than the odd name, "Parole," painted in large letters on green highway signs, today not much remains of the original farmland where tens of thousands of Civil War soldiers waited for assignments and permission to leave. But what happened to the bodies of the prisoners who went missing, or the dead that were buried in secret shallow graves?

One's imagination tends to wonder what amount of human remains might rest beneath modern housing developments and highways,

This historic marker along Route 2 in Parole indicates the site of the Civil War encampment.

shopping centers and schools—which were built atop the ground that once had bustled with life, and which also witnessed a fair amount of sickness and death—in the area that was known as Camp Parole.

Zouaves, Clara Barton and Washington the Gambler

Before Parole became the holding center for thousands of wounded soldiers and former prisoners awaiting assignment, the area temporarily hosted one of the most colorful, but shortest serving Union units—the 53rd New York Infantry.

Known as the D'Epineuil's Zouaves, because of the unit's large number of foreign born troops, their arrival in Annapolis in November 1861 did not go unnoticed, mainly due to their distinctive uniforms—baggy blue trousers, flowing white blouses, short open trimmed jackets, yellow leggings, sashes and bright red fez hats with dangling yellow tassels. Apparently, the foreign troops' rowdy behavior complemented their colorful costumes. The entire unit of loud, gambling, brawling soldiers often got drunk, and they were involved in fights throughout the camp. Eventually. the D'Epineuil's Zouaves left Annapolis, but their independent spirit caused War Department officials to disband the New York regiment in September 1862 and transfer its members to other units in the Union Army.

At Camp Parole, Clara Barton, known as the "Angel of the Battlefield," established her headquarters and cared for wounded Union troops. She later founded the American Red Cross. It's believed that the famous nurse probably worked with the wounded, or at least visited the temporary hospitals established at St. John's College and on the naval school's grounds.

The Parole area boasts one other distinction. It is the site of one of the country's oldest racetracks. It's believed that in the 1740s George Washington wagered several pounds on ponies at the track, and that he lost his investment.

Maryland's modern horse breeding and racing industries can trace their origins to the 18th-century racetrack that was established outside the capital city.

Currently, a major shopping complex named Annapolis Towne Center at Parole is under construction near the historic Parole Camp site. The large complex is expected to open in 2008.

*This drawing shows the layout at Camp Burnside, a Civil War training and parole campsite located near Annapolis. The image is dated Christmas Day 1861.*

The U.S. Naval Academy Chapel is the location of the crypt of America's naval hero John Paul Jones.

John Paul Jones' Final Resting Place

For more than a century the mortal remains of our first great sailor lay in an unknown grave lost to his country.

Thistory of a long journey, but certainly not one that was planned. And while there is no supernatural focus, the events illustrate that sometimes even the rich and famous have little control over the disposition of their personal assets—and, in particular, the selection of their final resting place.

There was a special ceremony held at the U.S. Naval Academy in Annapolis on July 9, 2005, marking the 100th anniversary of the return of the body of John Paul Jones from France, on July 22, 1905. But the route the American Revolutionary War naval hero took to arrive at his ornate marble crypt in his adopted country is one that spans two continents, an ocean and 113 years.

Jones is well known for uttering the most famous phrase in U.S. naval history—"I have not yet begun to fight."

His challenging reply occurred off the coast of England on Sept. 23, 1779, when a British captain demanded that the American sailor cease fire and surrender his sinking ship, the *Bonhomme Richard*. Jones ignored the enemy's demand and continued the battle. Although his ship was sunk, Jones and his brave crew were victorious, eventually capturing the British ship, HMS *Serapis*.

Born in Scotland on July 6, 1747, Jones came to the American colonies at the age of 26. He received a commission in the Continental Navy and commanded four ships. He never lost a battle and was known for his courage and warrior like spirit. However, when the Colonies defeated Great Britain, Jones longed for more action. So he followed the watery battlefields, serving in the navies of both Russia and France. On July 18, 1792, in failing health and relatively poor, he died in Paris.

In his book, *After the Funeral, The Posthumous Adventures of Famous Corpses*, Edwin Murphy details the long series of mishaps that occurred to the corpse of America's famed naval hero.

Since he had limited financial resources and was not extremely popular with some officials, Jones' death was ignored by the U.S. minister to France. The American sailor was buried in a Protestant cemetery about four miles outside of Paris. However, upon hearing of this indignity, the French government stepped in and gave Jones a hero's re-burial and preserved his corpse in alcohol in a lead coffin lined with straw.

Meanwhile, in the U.S., there seemed to be no interest in the fate of the late great hero, although a ship was named after Jones in 1834. In the late 1800s, a journalist began making inquires, and he learned that the rural site of the cemetery originally outside Paris had become part of the expanding city of Paris. Unfortunately for those seeking the naval hero's remains, buildings had long since devoured the general area of the

The final resting place of American naval hero John Paul Jones, whose body had been lost for more than 100 years in France

lost graveyard. According to *www.seacoastnh.com,* "The cemetery had been covered over by a grocery store, a laundry, an
apartment house, sheds, cess pools and wells."

Eventually, when the housing site was later condemned, an
excavation was conducted to locate the lost admiral, with workers spending weeks tunneling through old basements, caverns
and beneath the city's ancient streets. Much of the efforts to
locate and identify Jones' remains were led by General Horace
Porter, appointed American ambassador to France in 1899.

When five lead coffins were discovered, the records that
indicated Jones had been preserved in alcohol and tucked in
with straw helped the searches locate the correct lost corpse.
The body was discovered on April 8, 1905. Later, an autopsy and
a comparison of Jones remains—plus details of a bust created
years earlier by sculptor Jean-Antoine Houdon—confirmed the
remains to be those of the American naval officer.

With an American flag draped across a wooden coffin, Jones
was honored with a parade through Paris. At the port of
Cherbourg, nearly a dozen naval craft of both France and the
U.S. escorted the "Father of the American Navy" to his final rest-

ing place—a grand sepulcher
at the U.S. Naval Academy
chapel in Annapolis. Jones'
body arrived in Maryland on
July 22, 1905.

And there he waited, to
be buried, yet again.

Since Congress had not
appropriated the funds, there
was no waiting tomb, and
Jones' corpse sat in a storage
room in the basement of
Bancroft Hall for a year—
until the official, "welcome
home" ceremony, held on
April 24, 1906. On that day,
before a crowd of more than
a thousand, there were
speeches by the governor of
Maryland, who proclaimed

*Bust of the admiral, created by famed
sculptor Jean-Antoine Houdon*

Bancroft Hall is the largest dormitory in the country, housing approximately 4,000 midshipmen. The body of John Paul Jones was stored in the basement of this academy building while awaiting completion of his elaborate sarcophagus and crypt.

Jones was to rest in peace in the Old Line State; by the U.S. ambassador to France, who talked of the discovery and recovery of the long lost hero's body; and by U.S. President Theodore Roosevelt, who spoke of Jones' example and contributions to the Navy and the importance of a strong naval fleet. And the audience cheered.

And then Jones was hauled back into the basement of Bancroft Hall, for Congress still had not acted to approve funding for his crypt. It would be six years later, on Jan 26, 1913, when John Paul Jones had his final (fourth or fifth, but who's counting?) burial, in an ornate, marble sarcophagus, now located in the lower level of the Naval Academy chapel.

One would think that the story ends here, and for most people it does. But there are still some who question if the body in the magnificent mausoleum is really that of John Paul Jones. Some historians periodically suggest that the hallowed crypt be opened, and that a portion of the American hero's remains be compared with that of Jones' siblings, whose burial sites are known—just to be sure.

In one report, a Naval Academy spokesperson is said to have stated there is no question regarding the identity of the corpse, and that there are no plans to disturb the remains.

Most folks would tend to agree.

After all, shouldn't the poor restless sailor's soul rest in peace, at last?

Interesting facts:

In 1845, the Naval School was established with 50 students on 10 acres at the site of Fort Severn. By 1850, the name of the institution was changed to the U.S. Naval Academy. The complex has since grown to cover nearly 340 acres for training midshipmen.

The U.S. Naval Academy Chapel and its identifiable copper dome overlook the surrounding grounds of the academy and Maryland's adjacent capital city. The impressive house of worship was designed in 1904 by New York architect Ernest Flagg and dedicated in 1908. Tiffany Studios created many of the church's stained glass windows.

Memorabilia related to hero John Paul Jones—including replicas of his ships and his medals—are enclosed in displays surrounding the admiral's tomb. Visitors are able to access this circular walkway and view the detailed carvings on the crypt from all angles.

The statue of Indian chief Tecumseh, originally on the USS Delaware, *stands in front of Bancroft Hall. According to academy legend, the idol offers good luck to students, who toss pennies in its quiver before examinations to help ensure receiving a passing grade. The statue receives fresh coats of war paint before special occasions, such as football games and other major athletic contests and events.*

A bust created by Jean-Antoine Houdon is one of the pieces of art under glass along the walkway. Known as the sculpteur du roi (sculptor to the king). Houdon also completed busts of Benjamin Franklin, inventor Robert Fulton, emperor Napoléon Bonaparte, philosopher Jean-Jacques Rousseau and King Louis the XVI of France.

A plaque on the crypt wall states:

For more than a century the mortal remains of our first great sailor lay in an unknown grave lost to his country. The nation is indebted to General Horace Porter for his patriotic efforts in the discovery and identification of the body.

On a hallway at the entrance of the crypt, a dark brass plate preserves the following words:

Every officer in our navy should know by heart the deeds of John Paul Jones. Every officer in our navy should feel in each fiber of his being the eager desire to emulate the energy, the professional capacity, the indomitable determination and dauntless scorn of death which marked John Paul Jones above all his fellows.
—President Theodore Roosevelt

The interior of the Naval Academy Chapel features nautical images throughout the structure. Some of the stained glass windows were designed by Tiffany Studios.

Author Alex Haley's role as a storyteller is preserved in this sculpture located at the Annapolis dock near Market Space.

Sculpture Serves as a Reminder of the Past

Slaves were auctioned along the Annapolis docks and outside nearby taverns and later sent away to work on plantations throughout the South.

At the foot of Main Street, near the Market Space and along the edge of the dock, stand sculptures of four figures. The man represents Alex Haley, author of *Roots*, reading to three attentive children. The sculpture group was placed near the area where slaves arrived in America and were auctioned along the Annapolis docks and outside nearby taverns. Later they were sent to work on plantations throughout the South.

According to details on the Kunta Kinte-Alex Haley Foundation, Inc. web site, in 1981, a plaque placed at the site was dedicated, but it was stolen within two days after unveiling, allegedly by members of the Ku Klux Klan. Although the original plaque was never recovered, a replacement was installed within two months. The plaque reads:

To commemorate the arrival, in this harbor of Kunta Kinte, immortalized by Alex Haley in Roots, *and all others who came to these shores in bondage and who by their toil, character and ceaseless struggle for freedom have helped to make these United States.*

In 1767, Haley's ancestor, Kunta Kinte, is believed to have arrived at Annapolis City Dock on the slave ship *Lord Ligonier* and sold as a slave. Today, visitors are reminded of the late African-American author, who through his writing has educated countless people to the history and evils of slavery.

A pair of plaques stand in the edge of Annapolis' Brewer Hill Cemetery; one is dedicated to the memory of William Davis and Maryland's other victims of mob lynchings.

Ed Okonowicz

Christmas Week Lynching Near College Creek

'We will have to repent in this generation, not merely for the hateful words and actions of the bad people but the appalling silence of the good people.'
—Dr. Martin Luther King, Jr.

The rolling banks along College Creek in Annapolis are peaceful today. No groups stand on the St. John's College campus near the site of the Liberty Tree to protest British taxes on tea. The air is not filled with the singsong chants of auctioneers, selling slaves on auction blocks along the city's ancient docks. No cries of pain come from injured soldiers nursing wounds during the Civil War in field hospitals and temporary infirmaries.

Those times are gone, disappeared with the conflicts and ways of life that existed during various periods of the capital city's long and colorful history.

Today tourists and students, merchants and politicians, cross the attractive bridges that span the narrow waterways flowing through the historic town. A hilly cemetery borders the water's edge along College Creek.

But if those silent souls could speak, what stories they might tell—not only of what they experienced during life, but of what their spirits may have seen and heard just over a century ago, on a dark, bitter winter night when the old Maryland town was anything but calm and quiet.

Christmas Season

It was the blessed holiday season, 101 years ago in Maryland's capital city. Shoppers were buying presents, trees were selected for decoration and each family member's Sunday best had been laid out for the upcoming religious services. Within the week, pious churchgoers and once-a-year-attendees would kneel beside one another to celebrate Peace on Earth. But some local residents had ill intentions in mind, and an angry mob acted out its evil deeds on December 20, less than a week before Christmas Day.

That's when Henry Davis was pulled from the Annapolis jail on Calvert Street, dragged through town past St. John's College and hanged on the banks of College Creek.

The Friday morning, Dec. 21, 1906, edition of Baltimore's *The Sun* newspaper detailed the series of events that would place a black mark on the state's capital city and draw national attention to the mob crime—that resulted, to no one's surprise, in not a single arrest.

A series of stacked bold headlines offered readers all the major events associated with the lengthy front-page story that filled the paper's right-hand column.

In classic Victorian-era prose, the 1906 news article offered considerable detail. The unnamed correspondent's story is printed on the next page. However, while the article has been edited for clarity, the gruesome details remain to illustrate the barbaric nature of the mob's action and to show the role newspapers played in both informing, and to a degree, entertaining their subscribers during the early years of the 20th century.

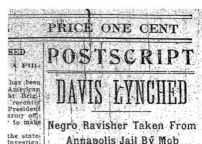

PRICE ONE CENT

POSTSCRIPT

DAVIS LYNCHED

Negro Ravisher Taken From Annapolis Jail By Mob And Hanged.

HE CONFESSED HIS CRIME

Declared He Intended To Murder As Well As Assault.

BODY RIDDLED WITH BULLETS.

Still Quivering It Was Cut Down And Left On Ground—Mob Included 25 Active Members And About 50 Others.

[Special Dispatch to the Baltimore Sun.] Annapolis, Md., Dec. 21, 3 A. M.—Battering down the doors of the Annapolis jail last night a determined mob took Henry

DAVIS LYNCHED

Annapolis, Md., Dec. 21, 3 A.M.—Battering down the doors of the Annapolis Jail last night a determined mob took Henry Davis, alias Chambers, from his cell, dragged him a quarter of a mile from the town, hanged him to the limb of an oak tree, riddled his body with bullets, then cut him down and left the quivering body on the ground.

The lynching occurred about 2:55 o'clock this morning.

Davis confessed a criminal assault upon Mrs. John Reid, of Iglehart's Station, last Friday.

Just before being hanged he said that it had been his determination to kill Mrs. Reid if he had not accomplished his purpose while she was alive.

In the jail were two extra deputy sheriffs, recently stationed there, and two watchmen. In addition the door had been barricaded with heavy timbers, in anticipation of possible attack. The mob, however, when a ruse failed, broke in the door with sledgehammers and axes, overpowered the guard and took the prisoner out . . . .

According to the story of an eyewitness, the mob was not unexpected. About 1:30 A.M. a number of men living near the Reid home came into town and talked lynching. They were joined by a number of townspeople, both responsible and irresponsible, until the actual participants numbered about 40. The onlookers increased the crowd to about 75.

They Try Ruse

Marching quietly to the jail, six of the men approached the door and rapped. Asked who they were, the men replied they were the sheriff with a prisoner. The watchman, not to be so easily fooled, flashed the electric light above the door and saw they were strangers.

The men then demanded the prisoner, and, after being refused, procured sledges and axes and returned. The deputies warned them that they would shoot if the mob persisted, but the men proceeded with their work of battering down the doors.

As the door fell in, a score of men covered the defenders with their revolvers. Others ran to Davis' cell on the third floor in the rear. There they found the negro handcuffed. They dragged him out into the crowd and there was a howl of delight. Young men ran up to the trembling negro and struck him about the head and kicked him about the body.

In a few minutes stronger men prevailed and he was marched out to Brickyard Hill on the Annapolis, Baltimore and Washington railroad.

Here Davis was closely questioned and again admitted that he had criminally assaulted his victim, and repeated that he would have done it living or dead.

As he made his assertion, those who heard him raised a cry, a rope was quickly knotted and the noose slipped over his head.

Willing Hands Pulled Rope

By this time Davis was nearly unconscious from fright and the blows which had been rained upon him. While in this condition willing hands pulled the rope and Davis swung twitching from the oaken limb.

Almost before his feet had left the ground a revolver cracked and a bullet cut a gash through his scalp. It was the signal for general firing and at least 100 bullets must have riddled his body.

After a few minutes the body was cut down, and after a few skeptical ones examined it and a few took pieces of rope and cloth as souvenirs, the mob seemed to melt quietly into the night.

The jail, which was so successfully attacked, is in the negro quarter of the town and many of the blacks fled from the town fearing they would be attacked. Those who stayed openly said they thought Davis received a just punishment.

Sheriff Joshua Linthicum arrived at the jail after the lynching, but would make no statement over the telephone. It was said among those who loitered about the town during the early evening hours discussing the situation that the defenders of the jail had said after the prisoner had been taken out that they determined to hold the door as long as possible, but not to wound any white man in defense of a negro . . . ."

[End of article]

According to the rest of the story, the victim of the assault was Mrs. Annie L. Reid, 48 years old, who lived about five miles from Annapolis. She reported she was attacked about a mile from her home. She said her attacker had threatened to kill her. When apprehended, Davis confessed the crime and said "the devil" prompted him to do it.

Ledger Readers Speak

During the weeks following the lynching, the *African American Ledger,* a weekly Baltimore newspaper, published columns and letters condemning both the criminal acts of the convict Davis and the mob rule. However, some readers asked appropriate questions about the ability of a mob to conduct such a lawless act in the state capital, with no apparent consequences.

One letter writer stated:

"A week or so ago . . . a mob of men assembled in the hall of a college near the vicinity, a State college at that, black them-selves up to make themselves look like black folks, and cover their faces with masks and proceed to the prison, take out the alleged criminal and hang and shoot him to death.

"Every detail from the time the mob assembled to the time the Negro is hanged and the mob disperses is known to the public by way of the newspapers. Not the slightest detail is left out . . . . Now we ask in the name of all that is good and true, if any one person who was present and able to give all these

Today the area near College Creek is calm and scenic. Years ago, some-where along the water's edge, it was the scene of mob violence and death.

95

details to the public press why was not that person able to give the names of those engaged in the murder of probably an innocent man.

"Up to the present the verdict of the coroner's jury stands: 'that the deceased came to his death at the hands of persons unknown to the jury.' This may be true, but we do not believe a word of it. If the persons were not known to the jury why were they not? . . . Why have there been no arrests? Why was not the newspaper correspondent summoned? He seems to have all the details, was it not possible for him to have shed some light on the matter, or was he immune from being questioned in the interest of justice?

"A number of people saw that something was going on and strange to say none of them manifested interest to inquire the meaning of a mob on the streets of such a quiet town as Annapolis, where a loud voice on the streets after a certain hour would certainly be enough to cause inquiry under ordinary cir-cumstances . . . . And yet only a passing notice is taken of the whole matter when the strictest investigation should have at once been put on foot to know why these people were there. Such innocence on the part of constituted authorities is almost beyond comprehension. It is absolutely incomprehensible and beyond conception that such innocence should exist outside of an infant asylum. But why say more?"

Davis Memorial Plaque

Lynchings—executions by mobs—occurred throughout the country, primarily in the southern and western states into the early 20th century. At times, traveling photographers took photo-graphs of the victims, sometimes hanging above a posing mob. In several instances, the faces of people in the crowd were uncovered and able to be identified in newspaper and postcard photographs. However, rarely were individuals charged and con-victed for participation in this form of mob justice.

According to the Maryland Archives web page, Davis was buried in the smallpox section of Brewer Hill Cemetery on West Street. The African-American graveyard, adjacent to Annapolis National Cemetery, is the resting place for former slaves, free blacks and U.S. Colored Troops, whose military gravestones bear the distinctive U.S.C.T. designation.

Near a chainlink fence on the west boundary of Brewer
Hill, stand two brass plaques with gold lettering. Dedicated on
December 20, 2001, one commemorates the execution of John
Snowden in 1919. The adjacent memorial honors the memory of
Davis and all Maryland victims of mob justice.

The plaque reads:

WHO WAS HENRY DAVIS?

Maryland Lynchings
The Record of Lynchings in Maryland from 1891-1906

May 13, 1891, Asbury Green, Centerville
May 17, 1892, James Taylor, Chestertown
June 8, 1893, Isaac Kemp, Princess Anne
October 20, 1894, Stephen Williams, Prince George's County
March 16, 1885, Marshall E. Price, Caroline County
March 28, 1895, Jacob Henson, Howard County
November 16, 1895, James Brown, Frederick
June 9, 1897, William Andrews, Princess Anne
May 25, 1898, Garfield King, Salisbury
December 21, 1906, Henry Davis, Annapolis

Henry Davis was the last man lynched in Annapolis,
on the day that he was lynched, the *Evening Capital* wrote,
"Annapolis and Anne Arundel County was given a black eye last night
by the lynching of the negro Davis . . ."
This memorial is dedicated to all the victims of lynchings.
May those who visit this site, be reminded that mob rule must never
become the law of the land.

The Annapolis dock area (center) and nearby Spa Creek (at right) have witnessed minor and significant historic events of the city, including a famous tea party protest, shipwrecks, riots and both the arrival and departure of thousands of ships carrying cargo, troops and slaves.

Tea Party and Riot
Along Quiet Spa Creek

In Annapolis, however, they didn't simply toss the tea overboard. In late October 1774, furious citizens caused an entire ship to be burned, along with more than 2,300 pounds of the 'detestable weed tea' that was on board.

T he calm waters of Spa Creek, at the foot of Compromise Street, separating the center of Annapolis from nearby Eastport, seem calm today. Boaters sail the historic waterway and tourists take pictures, enjoying the beauty of the shoreline, featuring historic homes and colorful watercraft.

Some visitors even think, for at least a fleeting moment, "I wish I could afford to live here, in such a peaceful, beautiful place." But serenity and beauty were not always associated with Spa Creek. During eras when waterways were the equivalent to today's interstate highways, some events along the waterway were anything but peaceful.

Annapolis Tea Party

In 1773, England passed a series of restrictive laws. These acts imposed additional taxes on British subjects, and they were opposed by most of the colonists.

In Boston Harbor, on Dec. 16, 1773, a group of up to 200 patriots—called the Sons of Liberty, and disguised as Indians—descended upon the city wharf hooting war chants. With thousands of citizens standing nearby, the patriots boarded three ships belonging to the East India Co., split open the crates filled with tea and tossed more than 300 chests into the harbor. Dubbed the "Boston Tea Party," news spread to other colonies and some imitated the actions and sent a defiant message to the

99

British government—protesting the issue of British government taxation without giving the American colonies representation. In retribution, British troops closed Boston Harbor, demanding that the citizens pay for the destroyed tea.

Both the issue of taxation and the reprisals on the citizens of Boston angered residents of the other colonies, and the actions of the Sons of Liberty and the issue of taxation became unifying themes and caused protests to spread. Throughout the individual colonies, many citizens refused to sell, buy or drink British tea.

Like the Boston Tea Party, the citizens of Chestertown, Md., demonstrated their opposition to England, but they did it during daylight—and without using disguises. In May 1774, angry citizens boarded a British ship loaded with tea and tossed the cargo into the Chester River.

In Annapolis, however, they didn't simply toss the tea overboard. In late October 1774, furious citizens caused an entire ship to be burned, along with more than 2,300 pounds of the "detestable weed tea" that was on board.

During the mounting opposition against England and the colonies' grassroots boycott against imported tea, Anthony

Colonial patriots threatened the owner of the Peggy Stewart House, shown in this old photograph, with personal injury and destruction of his home. At right is the house as it looks today.

Stewart's ship, the *Peggy Stewart*, which he had named after his daughter, arrived in Annapolis harbor. When people learned that the vessel's cargo contained tea, which the owner was intending to sell secretly, officials and townspeople organized to punish the merchant—threatening him with death and also destruction of his home and store. In addition to an apology and burning the cargo, the angry crowd at a public meeting demanded that the owner torch his own ship. The owner boarded the *Peggy Stewart* and set fire to the ship in full view of the town dock, where "a great number" of patriotic citizens gathered to watch the tea and the *Peggy Stewart* burn.

According to some, Stewart was forced to remain at the dock and watch his ship's destruction. Soon afterwards, he left the colony and settled with his family in England. But the charred remains of his *Peggy Stewart* rest at the bottom of Spa Creek, an unseen, but very memorable, symbol of the Annapolis Tea Party and Maryland's revolutionary spirit.

Francis Blackwell Mayer's (1827-1899) oil painting, depicting "The Burning of the *Peggy Stewart*" hangs in the Maryland State House. The historic piece of artwork, painted in 1896, is 72" x 53" and is on display in the Maryland Silver Room.

July Holiday Riot

You might say fireworks of a different kind were the talk of the town during the 1847 July Fourth celebration in Annapolis. On July 5, the excursion steamboat *Jewess*, under command of Captain Sutton, left Baltimore, heading for St. Michaels.

According to details provided in *The Ancient City, a History of Annapolis, in Maryland, 1649-1887*, by author Elihu S.Riley, a problem arose when the craft, with a full load of 700 civilian passengers, also squeezed on a number of military riflemen. These troops were heading for Talbot County, on the Eastern Shore, to participate in that area's holiday celebration.

After overloading the old craft, Capt. Sutton, who was concerned for the safety of his passengers realized he would not be able to cross the bay with all aboard. Therefore, after he had been on the water about five hours, the skipper made an unscheduled stop at Annapolis. His plan was to deposit about 150 passengers in the capital city and proceed with the troops and remaining civilians to his original destination. Unfortunately, no one wanted to leave the *Jewess*, particularly when the passengers learned they would have to head back to Baltimore as best they were able.

With the ship tied to the Annapolis dock, and with no quick resolution possible, a number of the Baltimoreans went

St. Mary's Church towers over Spa Creek. The waterway was anything but peaceful during July 1847, when Annapolis citizens and visitors from Baltimore confronted each other along the dock.

into town to enjoy the day and take in the sights. What happened next, depends upon which version of the story you read.

The capital city residents gave the impression their quiet town had been invaded, and they found the Baltimoreans disorderly and disruptive as they wandered throughout the city. The steamboat tourists, however, claimed Annapolis folks were both inhospitable and threatening.

Tempers flared and tension escalated to a dangerous level. At first, fruits were tossed from the boat at a mob gathered along shore. The Annapolitans responded by throwing bricks at the *Jewess* passengers. This caused the soldiers on board to grab their rifles and aim them at the angry faces on the dock.

With Captain McAllister, commander of the riflemen, waving his sword at the crowd, and town leaders trying to calm the hometown mob, shots were fired—nearly two dozen from the steamboat and several pistol and rifle shots coming from shore. After the smoke cleared, the score ended up Baltimore-FIVE, Annapolis-ZERO—with five capital residents wounded on shore and no visiting tourists injured on board the boat.

Bullets had struck several Annapolitans, striking some in the legs, thigh and side. One man lost two toes. According to one eyewitness, "The people on board the boat hurrahed enough for an election day," when they saw two of the rock throwers struck by the ship's riflemen.

As word of the escalating battle circulated through town, well-intentioned citizens took positions along the creek and some were aiming their weapons at the passengers on the *Jewess*. Thankfully, the self-appointed snipers did not fire on the ship, which was struggling to get away from shore and distance itself from the angry mob.

To avenge the town's honor and help protect their fellow citizens, several well-meaning patriots rolled the town cannon to the dock and prepared to fire at the steamboat. A town judge struggled against the mob members who tried several times to fire the deadly weapon, which the judge had been able to disable with a toothpick.

Apparently, the overloaded craft escaped from Spa Creek and the mob dispersed. A subsequent investigation resulted in no arrests and no proceedings against anyone who was in the town or aboard the visiting steamboat that early July.

Somewhere in the snowy woods in St. Mary's County is the site of the death of Moll Dyer, the county's most famous witch.

Tales and Legends of Witchcraft in Maryland

In 1654, Mary Lee was hanged as a witch at sea by the crew of the vessel Charity. *Her crime . . . bearing a skin imperfection that the ship's authorities decided was 'the mark of the Devil.'*

Because of its infamous 1692 Witch Trials, Salem, Massachusetts, has cornered the market as the recognized historical center of witchcraft in America. But accepted fact can be deceiving. Maryland, like other colonies in the early days of America's settlement, had its own witch trials. There are reports and legends associated with women and men, who were accused of possessing supernatural powers and who were associates and assistants of the Devil.

Sarah the Witch

In his book *Annapolis: Three Centuries of Glamour,* author Elmer M. Jackson Jr., tells the tale of a ship named the *Lovely Nancy,* which was completed by a local shipbuilding firm and scheduled to be launched into the nearby river. As was always the case, a large crowd had gathered to witness the special event and participate in the festivities. Among those in the crowd was an old fortuneteller believed to dabble in the mysterious. Many considered the old woman named Sarah McDonald a "witch."

As the ship was christened and began to slide down the ramp toward the water, the crowd cheered. But the excited anticipation gave way to silence and concern, for the craft stopped in mid descent and, despite the efforts of the men in the crowd, did not move any further. Later, word circulated through the town that earlier in the day Sarah had cursed the ship and the event, for she had been overheard saying, "The *Lovely Nancy* will not see water today."

When the ship's captain and boat builders heard about Sarah's involvement, they threatened to duck the old woman in the nearby water beside the ship until she withdrew the powerful spell. Wisely, old Sarah went into hiding and did not reappear in town until after the ship had been launched successfully a few days later.

Today, of course, such a mild comment as Sarah's would not cause the same reaction. Rather than be taken seriously, the connection of the statement and resulting action would be ignored or accepted as mere coincidence. But in the 17th and 18th centuries, simple remarks, unexplained events and physical deformities could result in legal charges, physical punishment and even death.

Here are only a few reasons that could cause one to be branded suspicious, and end up on trial for one's life:

> Acting or appearing strange
> Talking to a farm animal or pet
> Owning a broomstick
> Using herbs to cure illness
> Speaking in a strange language
> Growing a good crop
> Having a bad crop
> Gazing at a neighbor with ill intent
> Arguing with a well-respected citizen—especially a politician landowner or member of the clergy
> Avoiding contact with other villagers
> Consorting with the "Devil" or
> Bearing the "mark of the Devil"

The so-called bad luck "mark" could be anything from an obvious physical handicap or speech impediment to a small mole or simple birthmark. In 1654, Mary Lee was hanged as a witch at sea by the crew of the vessel *Charity*. Her crime, apparently, was being in the wrong place at the wrong time and bearing a skin imperfection that the ship's authorities decided was "the mark."

Unlucky Mary Lee

Unfortunately for Mary Lee, the ship she had boarded in England, bound for Maryland, had been subjected to a series of fierce Atlantic storms. According to two articles—Loring Wilson's "The Devil You Say" and Jack O'Brien's "Which Witch Is Which?" —for nearly two months, the ship, crew and passengers suffered from the damaging beating of high waves. Eventually, someone suggested that such horrible weather could only be the result of one thing: A witch was on board the *Charity*.

One of the passengers was a religious man, and he agreed to examine all of the women on the vessel. Afterwards, he announced that Mary Lee bore the unclean "mark."

Looking for any possible way to stop the endless rough weather, the crew and passengers hanged the selected woman from the tallest wooden mast. After a suitable period of time— during which her dangling corpse served as an example of what would become of any other aspiring witches hiding aboard the *Charity*—the mob tossed Mary Lee's vile body and every trace of her tainted belongings overboard. They hoped that the human sacrifice would satisfy the angry sea gods.

Miraculously, the storm ceased immediately. This sudden and positive result confirmed to the participants that their suspicions about Mary Lee were correct, and that their actions, which solved the weather problem, were entirely justified. Certainly, it was a classic example of the "end justifying the means."

But poor Mary Lee's situation was only one of hundreds of "witchcraft" incidents reported throughout many of the newfound Colonies.

In *Historical Witches and Witchtrials in North America,* complied by Marc Carlson, there are scores of instances of witchcraft accusations and trials. They occurred in New England, the mid-Atlantic, the Deep South and even the far Western territories. And while ducking, whipping, being burned at the stake, imprisoned and shunned are the more common punishments, the most unusual disposition of a witch occurred in Salem in 1692. That's when Giles Corey was pressed to death after refusing repeatedly to agree to offer a plea to accusations he was involved in the practice of sorcery.

In the counties surrounding the Chesapeake Bay, there were a number of recorded cases related to witchcraft.

In 1654, Mrs. Richard Manship was accused of witchcraft, but she was not convicted, and her accuser, Peter Godson, was judged to have defamed and slandered her.

In 1658, the crew of the ship *Sarah Artch* hanged Elizabeth Richardson at sea as a witch.

In 1661, Joan Mitchell, in Charles County, was accused of witchcraft and brought suit against four people for slandering her.

In 1665, Elizabeth Bennett, of Saint Mary's County, was accused of witchcraft and acquitted.

In 1674, John Cowman, of Saint Mary's County, was convicted of witchcraft, conjuration, sorcery or enchantment on the body of Elizabeth Goodale, but he received a reprieve from execution—while standing on the gallows with a noose around his neck.

In 1685, Rebecca Fowler, of Calvert County, was executed for witchcraft.

In 1686, Hannah Edwards, of Calvert County, was acquitted of witchcraft.

In 1702, Katherine Prout, of Charles County, was charged as being a witch and fined 100 pounds of tobacco.

In 1712, Virtue Violl, of Talbot County, a spinster, was acquitted of the charge of witchcraft.

Moll Dyer

In St. Mary's County, some long-time residents associate any mention of witchcraft with the local legend of "Moll Dyer." The story of her horrible death and a mysterious curse has been passed down orally for generations, and it remains a strong part of the region's local history and folklore. Although centuries have passed since the woman's death, St. Mary's County Historical Society in Leonardtown displays a rock that's believed to be a tangible link with the eerie figure.

In the late 1600s, Moll Dyer lived in an unsightly hut in the forest—away from townsfolk. She was a hermit—odd looking, old, not sociable and downright scary.

Those being superstitious times, the accepted and respected citizens didn't associate with the likes of Moll. And when bad things happened—such as a freak storm, ruined crops, unexplained deaths and accidents or a dried-up cow—blaming Moll, who was a bit eccentric, seemed to be a good idea.

Remember, these were days when nearly two-dozen folks were executed for witchcraft in Salem, Massachusetts. Maryland historical records indicate at least 12 cases where persons were accused of witchcraft—and there also were witch trials held in Pennsylvania and Virginia.

To solve the community's problems, the respected locals decided to burn Moll out of her secluded home. They thought this would drive her from the area and cause her to reside elsewhere—where she could ruin someone else's crops and dry up other farmers' cows.

In the middle of a windy winter night, a group of men crept through the woods and set fire to Moll's dwelling. Escaping the flames, Moll fled into the forest and hid. The mob went back to town, thinking their problems with Moll were over. Several days passed, and there was no sign of the dreaded witch. But soon a young boy, who had been walking in the woods, came into

The rock, located to the far right, beside the St. Mary's County Historical Society building, was moved from the site in the forest where it is believed the witch Moll Dyer died.

town and reported finding Moll's dead, frozen body. It was kneeling beside a rock, with one hand raised, as if in a state of prayer. The dead witch's other hand rested on the small boulder.

It's said witch Moll Dyer left her hand print on the right side of this rock, which was moved into Leonardtown, beside the county historical society building.

As news spread of her discovery, the townsfolk were relieved, initially. But then unexplained events and bad luck returned to the area. Animals died and there were sudden, fierce storms. Floods and illness seemed to take up residence in St. Mary's County. It was as if Moll Dyer had cursed her attackers and all the other residents.

Then someone noticed an imprint on the boulder, upon which the witch's corpse had been resting when her body had been found. And the mark seemed to be an impression of a handprint in the stone, as if Moll had died praying that the curse she directed upon her killers would remind the town of her power and their murderous deed.

Over time, the stream near her burned out hut became known as Moll Dyer Run. Today Moll Dyer Road is another reminder of the area's resident witch.

Of course, nighttime travelers had reported seeing a ghost-like figure roaming the area. And there have been reports that, on the coldest night of each year, the spirit of Moll returns to the area where her hut had stood, and also to the rock upon which she had died.

The famous rock was found and moved, on Oct. 14, 1972, to the Old Jail in Leonardtown, which houses the St. Mary's County Historical Society. Visitors are able to examine the 875-lb. rock, which is located beside the Old Jail, and many try to locate and take pictures of the impression of Moll's hand and fingers.

Blair Witch

Any chapter about Maryland witches would be incomplete without at least a mention of the state's most modern legend. In 1999, the topic of witchcraft in Maryland moved beyond historical documents, legends and folklore, At that time, publicity surrounding the movie, *The Blair Witch Project,* overshadowed historical witchcraft events, and Maryland's Blair Witch became one of the newest eerie characters added to the pages of American folklore. However, the entire story of the vengeful peasant who killed the town's children and cursed the area around Burkittsville, in Frederick County, was fiction.

A few creative filmmakers, who made millions of dollars on the fabricated tale, developed the legend. Their story remains a classic example of regional fakelore and a significant illustration of the power of blatant commercialization—proving the enduring popularity of both historical and legendary witches and things that go bump in the night.

And some still believe—or want to believe—in the existence of women in black capes, who ride at night on broomsticks and who live in wooded areas, possess magical powers and cast spells—especially in late October.

SOURCES

INTERVIEWS
Lively, Carter C., Hammond-Harwood House
O'Brien, Lynn, Brice House
Schatz, Mark, Ann Arrundell Historical Society, Inc.

BOOKS
Anderson, Elizabeth B., ANNAPOLIS: *A Walk Through History.* *Centreville*, MD; Tidewater Publishers, 1984

Brugger, Robert J., *Maryland: A Middle Temperament, 1634-1980.* Baltimore, MD; The Johns Hopkins University Press, 1988

Force, Peter, *A Documentary History of the English Colonies in North America, from The King's Message to Parliament, of March 7, 1774 to The Declaration of Independence by The United States.* Washington, D.C; M. St. Clair Clark and Peter Force, 1839

Hauck, Dennis William, *The National Directory of Haunted Places.* New York, NY; Penguin Books, 1996

Jackson, Elmer M. Jr., *Annapolis: Three Centuries of Glamour.* Annapolis, MD; The Capital-Gazette Press, 1936

Johnston, George, *History of Cecil County, Maryland.* Baltimore, MD; Genealogical Publishing Co., Inc., 1989

Legends of St. Mary's: A collection of haunts, witches and other strange occurrences. St. Mary's County Historical Society

Lake, Matt, *Weird Maryland.* New York, NY; Sterling Publishing Company Inc., 2006

Maryland: A New Guide to the Old Line State. Editors, Papenfuse, Edward C.; Stiverson, Gregory A.; Collins, Susan A.; and Carr, Lois Green. Baltimore, MD; The Johns Hopkins University Press, 1976

Moose, Katie, *Annapolis: The Guide Book.* Annapolis, MD; Conduit Press, 2001

Okonowicz, Ed, *Baltimore Ghosts: History, Mystery, Legends and Lore.* Elkton, MD; Myst and Lace Publishers Inc., 2004

Okonowicz, Ed, *Crying in the Kitchen.* Elkton, MD; Myst and Lace Publishers Inc., 1998

Okonowicz, Ed, *Haunted Maryland.* Mechanicsburg, PA; Stackpole Books, 2003

Riley, Elihu S., *The Ancient City, a History of Annapolis, in Maryland, 1649-1887.* Annapolis, MD; Record Printing Office, 1887

ARTICLES

Obituary of Russian Sailor, Demidoff, *Annapolis Gazette*, February 11, 1864

"Anniversary of return of Jones' remains marked," *The Daily Banner*, July 9, 2005

Arcieri, Katie, "Parole development rising from the dirt: Construction on area's first Target begins," *The Capital*, Feb. 11, 2007

Blake, Allison, "Ghosts give 'living history' new meaning," *The Capital*, November 1998

Bragdon, Julie, "The Unseen Presence: Ghosts In Annapolis," *Annapolis Magazine*, October 1984

Burdett, Hal, "Brice House ghost stories," *Evening Capital*

"Celebrated Brice House Ghosts Now Believed Gone: New Owners Haven't Seen Single One," *Evening Capital*, October 31, 1957

Duke, Jacqueline, "Historic haunting ground," *The Capital*, October 30, 1982

"Get spooked!—Halloween is a great time to meet the ghosts of Annapolis," *The Publick Enterprise*, October 1994

"Ghosts (Civil War Nurses?) haunt St. J. dormitory," *Anne Arundel Times*

Hill, Mark, "Are All the Witches Gone from Maryland? From the 1650s Until 50 Years Ago, Witchcraft Was Known Here"

Manger, Dyan, "Ghosts Haunt Annapolis," *Annapolitan*, October 1973

Mellin, John, "Who says Parole was prison camp?" *The Capital*, February 8, 1990

Oakey, Jane and King, Terry, "Do spooks feel the cold in Annapolis? Ghost House Undergoes Renovation," *Anne Arundel Times*, February 15, 1979

O'Brien, Jack, "Which Witch Is Which?"

"Parole, Former Civil War Troop Encampment Site and Racetrack"

Peniston, Bradley, "Local Haunts, Guided ghost tours unearth Annapolis' haunted history," *Sunday Capital*, October 23, 1994

Reppert, Ralph, "Parole, Maryland"

"The Curtis Creek Furnace and Iron Works," Ann Arrundell County Historical Society, Inc. document

Waters, Sarah, "The Otherworldly Side of St. John's," student paper by 1988 graduate provided by St. John's College Communications Office

Wilson, Becky, "The Whistler—and the wayward elevator," *Diversions, The Wide World of Other*, November 1982

Wilson, Loring D., "The Devil You Say"

ONLINE SOURCES

General Information about Annapolis and Maryland
http://www.msa.md.gov/msa/homepage/html/homepage.html
http://funkmasterj.tripod.com/mdf.htm
http://marylandghosts.com/

Annapolis National Cemetery
http://www.cem.va.gov/CEM/cems/nchp/annapolis.asp
http://famousamericans.net/theodoreohara/
http://www.navpooh.com/oldindex.html
http://www.cem.va.gov/pdf/Annap.pdf

Brice House
http://www.annapolis.org/
http://www.bsos.umd.edu/anth/aia/james_brice_house.htm

Governor's Bridge
http://www.realhaunts.com/united-states/governors-bridge/
http://www.snopes.com/horrors/madmen/hook.asp

Hammond-Harwood House
http://www.hammondharwoodhouse.org/

John Paul Jones and U.S. Naval Academy
http://www.seacoastnh.com/jpj/burial.html
http://www.usna.edu///homepage.php
http://www.southcoastsar.org/Rcvry_JPJ.htm

Kunta Kinte Monument
http://www.mdslavery.net/
http://www.kuntakinte.com/memorialelements.html#wall
http://www.annapolis.gov/info.asp?page=1717

Lynching of Henry Davis
http://ecpclio.net/megafile/msa/speccol/sc5300/sc5339/000070/000000/0
00044/restricted/0006.html
http://www.msa.md.gov/msa/speccol/sc3500/sc3520/013600/013635/htm
l/msa13635.html

Peggy Stewart
http://www.seakayak.ws/kayak/kayak.nsf/NavigationList/NT00435C42
http://www.answers.com/topic/peggy-stewart

Parole, Maryland
http://www.civilwararchive.com/Unreghst/unnyinf5.htm#53re
http://www.geocities.com/naforts/md.html
http://www.pa-roots.com/~pacw/campparole.html
http://www.bayweekly.com/year04/issuexii18/leadxii18.html
http://www.cem.va.gov/pdf/Annap.pdf

St. John's College
http://www.stjohnscollege.edu/asp/home.aspx
http://www.stjohnscollege.edu/asp/main.aspx?page=6591&parent=1106#alumni
http://www.sos.state.md.us/mmmc/FrenchMon.htm

Thomas Dance and Maryland State House
http://www.bayweekly.com/year01/issue9_43/lead9_43.html
http://www.msa.md.gov/msa/stagser/s1259/131/html/tour.html
http://www.msa.md.gov/msa/homepage/html/statehse.html
http://www.hometownannapolis.com/tour_statehouse.html
http://www.msa.md.gov/msa/stagser/s1259/121/5847/html/dome4000.html

Witches in North America and Maryland
http://www.personal.utulsa.edu/~marc-carlson/witchtrial/na.html

About the Author

Ed Okonowicz is a storyteller and a regional author of books on Mid-Atlantic culture, oral history, folklore and ghost stories. As a part time instructor, he teaches folklore and storytelling at the University of Delaware. In 2005 he was voted Best Local Author in *Delaware Today* magazine's Readers' Poll. His two books on *Possessed Possessions: Haunted Antiques, Furniture and Collectibles* led him to appear in October 2005, with psychic James Van Praagh on The Learning Channel two-hour special, *Possessed Possessions*, filmed on the *Queen Mary*.

Annapolis GHOSTS is a follow up to his book *Baltimore GHOSTS: History, Mystery, Legends and Lore. Haunted Maryland* and *Gold, Frankincense and Myrrh,* his Christmas novel, will be released in 2007.

About the Artist/Designer

Kathleen Okonowicz, a watercolor artist, is responsible for all of the layout and book covers of Myst and Lace Publishers' publications. She is a member of the Baltimore Watercolor Society. Her artwork and prints are found at exhibitions and her web site www.mystandlace.com/gallery.html

In 2007, she announced her *Haunted Places* series, which features original paintings of historic and legendary mid-Atlantic sites.

TRUE
Ghost Stories from
Master Storyteller
Ed Okonowicz

*S*pirits *Between the Bays* Series

Wander through the rooms, hallways and dark corners of this eerie collection.

Creep deeper and deeper into terror, and learn about the area's history in our series of ghostly tales and folklore from states in the Mid-Atlantic region.

For detailed information on each volume, visit our web site.

$9.95 each

Visit our web site at: www.mystandlace.com

Lighthouse Legends, History and Lore

Lighthouses of New Jersey and Delaware
by Bob Trapani Jr.

128 pages
5 1/2" x 8 1/2"
softcover
ISBN 1-890690-15-5
$11.95

Shipwrecks, storms, suicides, rescues, ghost stories, unusual events and regional folklore are featured in this unique coastal history of the mid-Atlantic region. Bob Trapani Jr., executive director of the American Lighthouse Foundation, presents lighthouse history in an entertaining and storytelling fashion using historic and contemporary photographs, oral history, document research and personal experiences. From Sandy Hook to Cape May and from Fenwick Island through the Delaware Bay enjoy tales of that offer history in an entertaining fashion. *(Published in 2005)*

The author, Bob Trapani Jr., is executive director of the American Lighthouse Foundation, located in Wells, Maine.

Lighthouses of Maryland and Virginia
by Bob Trapani Jr.

Stories about light keepers and lighthouses of the Chesapeake Bay and Atlantic Coast are featured in this entertaining volume by lighthouse historian Bob Trapani Jr. From Assateague Island to Baltimore's Inner Harbor, from the Susquehanna Flats to the Virginia Coast, enjoy stories about the region's magical and mystical lights. *(Published in 2006)*

176 pages
5 1/2" x 8 1/2"
softcover
ISBN 1-890690-17-1
$11.95

Visit our web site at: www.mystandlace.com

Terrifying Tales of the Beaches and Bays
Volumes 1 and 2

In *Terrifying Tales of the Beaches and Bays* and the sequel, award-winning author and storyteller Ed Okonowicz shares eerie accounts of spirits roaming the mid-Atlantic beaches and shore.

128 pages
5 1/2" x 8 1/2"
softcover
ISBN 1-890690-06-6

$9.95 each

128 pages
5 1/2" x 8 1/2"
softcover
ISBN 1-890690-10-4

POSSESSED OBJECTS PLAGUE THEIR OWNERS

Read about them in *Possessed Possessions* and *Possessed Possessions 2* the books some antique dealers **definitely** do not want you to buy.

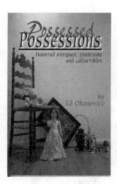

"If you're looking for an unusual gift for a collector of antiques, or enjoy haunting tales, this one's for you." —Collector Editions

"This book is certainly entertaining, and it's even a bit disturbing." —Antique Week

112 pages
5 1/2" x 8 1/2"
softcover
ISBN 0-9643244-5-8

$9.95 each

112 pages
5 1/2" x 8 1/2"
softcover
ISBN 0-890690-02-3

Visit our web site at: www.mystandlace.com

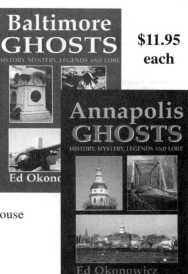

To Order our Books

Name _____

Address_____

City_____State_____Zip Code_____

Phone _(_____)_____e-mail:_____

To receive the free *Spirits Speaks* newsletter and information on future volumes, public tours and events, send us your e-mail address, visit our web site [www.mystandlace.com] or fill out the above form and mail it to us.

I would like to order the following books:

Quantity	Title	Price	Total
_____	**Annapolis Ghosts**	**$11.95**	_____
_____	**Haunted Maryland**	**$ 9.95**	_____
_____	Civil War Ghosts at Fort Delaware	$11.95	_____
_____	Baltimore Ghosts	$11.95	_____
_____	Baltimore Ghosts Teacher's Guide	$ 8.95	_____
_____	Lighthouses of Maryland and Virginia	$11.95	_____
_____	Lighthouses of New Jersey and Delaware	$11.95	_____
_____	Terrifying Tales of the Beaches and Bays	$ 9.95	_____
_____	Terrifying Tales 2 of the Beaches and Bays	$ 9.95	_____
_____	Treasure Hunting	$ 6.95	_____
_____	Opening the Door, Vol II (second edition)	$ 9.95	_____
_____	In the Vestibule, Vol IV	$ 9.95	_____
_____	Presence in the Parlor, Vol V	$ 9.95	_____
_____	Crying in the Kitchen, Vol VI	$ 9.95	_____
_____	Up the Back Stairway, Vol VII	$ 9.95	_____
_____	Horror in the Hallway, Vol VIII	$ 9.95	_____
_____	Phantom in the Bedchamber, Vol IX	$ 9.95	_____
_____	Possessed Possessions	$ 9.95	_____
_____	Possessed Possessions 2	$ 9.95	_____
_____	Ghosts	$ 9.95	_____
_____	Fired! A DelMarVa Murder Mystery (DMM)	$ 9.95	_____
_____	Halloween House (DMM#2)	$ 9.95	_____
_____	Disappearing Delmarva	$38.00	_____
_____	Friends, Neighbors & Folks Down the Road	$30.00	_____
_____	Stairway over the Brandywine, A Love Story	$ 5.00	_____

*Md residents add 5% sales tax.
  Please include $2.50 postage for the first book, and 50 cents for each additional book.
  Make checks payable to:
      Myst and Lace Publishers

Subtotal_____
Tax*_____
Shipping _____
Total _____

All books are signed by the author. If you would like the book(s) personalized, please specify to whom.   Mail to: Ed Okonowicz
                      1386 Fair Hill Lane
                      Elkton, Maryland 21921

Visit our web site at: www.mystandlace.com